THE LAW OF ATTRACTION

THE SECRET SAUCE OF SUCCESS IN GETTING LOVE, HEALTH, AND WEALTH

AJAY SINGH

Copyright © Ajay Singh
All Rights Reserved.

This book is dedicated to you, who seek emotional, physical, mental, financial, and spiritual well-being with upliftment in every area of your life. Manifesting this book in your hands is an evidence of your ability to align yourself with the universal energies and call forth the infinite creative powers. And now you will get any of your desires fulfilled post understanding the Law of Attraction at a deeper spiritual and scientific level.

This book is where you begin!

Contents

Foreword   *vii*

Acknowledgements   *ix*

1. Who Are We?   1

2. Thoughts And Emotions   7

3. The Law Of Attraction Is The Secret Sauce   19

4. Conscious And Subconscious Mind   39

5. Meditation And Alignment With Universal   53
   Energy

6. Intuition And Inspired Action   62

7. Setting Up Goals, Desires, And Intentions   70

8. Believe   82

9. Visualization   92

10. Affirmation   111

11. Vision Board   124

12. Journaling   132

13. Gratitude   140

14. Scientific Explanation Of Law Of Attraction   151

15. Manifesting Health   157

16. Manifesting Wealth   164

17. Manifesting Love   171

18. Manifesting Dream Career   181

19. Success In Parenting Using The Law Of   188
    Attraction

20. Helping Others Using The Law Of Attraction   194

Contents

About The Author   197

Foreword

The Law of Attraction is neither a recent discovery nor a new concept. If you approach this book with an open heart and an unprejudiced mind, you will learn that we all are the co-creators in the creation of our life experiences. You can then look back in your lives and clearly understand why you are like this and where you are today, in relation to where you wanted to really go. You will easily understand how you were creating your life experiences by default, because these principles work whether you know about them or not, just like gravity. You will then be able to wide your perception and use the universal principles to deliberately create the lives you want for your future. The purpose of your life is to seek joy and the inherent basis of your life is freedom. It is my hope that through the information and practices mentioned in this book, you will connect with your true self, with your inner being who always wants joy, prosperity, and abundance in your life. _The pages that you are about to read contain some of the most powerful teachings available on the planet today._

As you are now ready to read and apply this great wisdom, I urge you to stop after each chapter and absorb the pure energy that you will feel and see how every sentence resonates with you, as at the core of your being you have always known this. The way everything in life is happening will soon start making sense to you. You will find the content quite startling and yet so simple. This book also offers examples on the variety of subjects in which people often find themselves out of alignment with their own desires. I will discuss limiting beliefs around desires related to your health, relationships, career, and wealth etc. and will attempt to dissolve them right when you are reading about them and assist you in creating new positive beliefs. You are about to see and experience a whole new world changing right in front of your eyes. You will feel reconnection to the universal energy that creates worlds and manifests your dreams.

This is my desire that the information, examples, and the tools presented in this book helps you to align yourself with your true self and your desires for a happy and a fulfilling life. You can start from right where you are. No matter what your life looks like today, you can begin changing it for the better, right at this moment.

So now, just relax and enjoy the delicious unfolding of this book!

Acknowledgements

I wish to express my heartfelt gratitude to all the students and people who attended my Law of Attraction webinar and workshops and unknowingly helped this book to evolve with my experience and beautiful interactions with them at not just verbal but more at spiritual and energy level. These personal interactions have assisted me to understand and make this book easier for the reader to absorb and to put into immediate practical use. I have also learnt from all of you as learning is a continuous practice and together, we have experienced that we can't continue the same old habitual limiting thought patterns and get new unlimited results. You probably will notice some repetition in this book of key teachings, but remember we learn best through repetition! Rather then like any other entertaining fictional book, which you read, enjoy and keep aside – this is a book to be read, revisited, studied, and put into the practical use. This book is a manifestation of my desire and your desire, to assist you to get a fulfilling life in every aspect - be it Love, Health, Wealth, Career, Spirituality, or anything. I feel especially gratified that this book is now on its way to those who are asking the questions that it will answer!

Happy reading. This works beyond your imagination!

Who are we?

The non-physical part of us

For most of us, the physical body comes to the mind the moment we think of who we are. And it's obvious as it's easy to see the tangible. Till now you have known yourself as a three-dimensional figure mostly. But have you noticed that this body functions on its own, without your guidance and intervention? You don't have to instruct it to breathe, to make the heartbeat, to make the liver work and to make the nervous system do what it does. Everything that is happening in this most complex machine that we call our body is happening by itself. If you think in this way you will realize that there is something more associated with our identity, there is a super intelligence at work which beyond all logics is managing all the complex functions of our body. Think about it in this way, what will happen if all these functions are left to you to monitor and do - to breathe, to make the heartbeat and pump the blood to all the vital organs, to maintain the complex nervous system. It's impossible for us to manage and we will die in flat 30 seconds! Isn't it?

Now think of what possibilities you will have if you can have access to this infinite super intelligence consciously rather than unconsciously. Your all dreams and desires will come true magically. Unfortunately, most of us being not totally aware of this nonphysical dimension of us are living our lives in fear and thus sets lower goals in life. At the same time each one of us has a longing to expand, to become boundless as all of us at some level have some awareness that we are more than just physical. It's a natural desire in human beings to transcend the limitations of the physical.

"As a machine and as a platform for life, the human body is faultless. The only problem is that it does not take you anywhere; it springs out of the earth and falls back into it. Isn't that enough? At one level, it is quite enough. But somehow, a dimension beyond physicality has infused itself into this wonderful mechanism. This dimension is the very source of life. It is this that truly makes us who we are. In every creature, plant, and seed, this is at work. In a human being, this source of life is even more magnificently obvious. This is why human beings seem to live in a constant struggle between the physical and the dimension beyond. Though you have the compulsiveness of the physical, you also have the consciousness of being more than just physical."

- *Sadhguru Jaggi Vasudev*

To know the subtler realms of your own existence and to look beyond it needs pure and burning intention and tools like meditation, which makes you realize that you are a boundless source of creation in yourself and can create anything just by aligning your thoughts, emotions, and energies. As a human being if we look beyond just our needs of survival and have an intention to align with our inner being, then we can experience divine in our own inner being.

We are not the body and the mind

Currently we have limited our identifications just to our body and the mind. There are methods using which you can feel the presence of the sensory body which is beyond this physical body. Using them you can feel anything and everything as part of you. Through the practice of Yoga which means union, Indian yogis from ancient times have experienced the limitless expansion of their sensory body and felt the whole universe as part of them.

"We're all connected. We just don't see it. There isn't an 'out there' and an 'in here'. Everything in the universe is connected. It is just one energy field."

• *John Assaraf*

Many identify themself as mind, but again it's a false sense of identification. Mind is just your faculty to enable you to think, imagine and memorize, but you yourself are not mind. Once you get identified with something that you are not, you block your intelligence from further exploration.

Through practices like meditation, you will realize that everything is energy which as of now you have just read or heard since childhood. You will then start feeling your alignment with that universal energy which you may call God, infinite intelligence or your inner being. You and me, this book you are reading, the chair on which you are sitting, the trees around you, everything is energy, made up of atoms in constant motion. All matter is energy and energy can neither be created nor destroyed. Also, it never rests and is always moving from one form to another.

"Energy cannot be created or destroyed; it can only be changed from one form to another."

• *Albert Einstein*

You will feel a connection with everything and everyone after the self-realization that comes after practicing tools like meditation, gratitude, and prayer. The wisdom of the entire cosmos will be bestowed upon you without asking. The common coincidences which all of us had experienced like, on a particular day you were thinking of someone, whom you have not met or spoken to in months or years and the same day that person calls you. All such things you have known as coincidences till now will suddenly start making sense to you as the result of the Law of Synchronization due to which different events in your life have synchronized. Synchronization is the alignment of the same wavelength of energy. That is how the Law of Attraction works. We synchronize with similar frequencies. Quantum Physics has now started acknowledging such phenomenon.

"The day science begins to study non-physical phenomena; it will make more progress in one decade than in all the previous centuries of its existence."

- *Nikola Tesla*

Everything we experience in our outside reality is a reflection of our own energetic state. We therefore always create our experience with our own vibration, which we will discuss in upcoming chapters in more detail. For now, let's just understand that we literally are the living magnets and attract people, circumstances and events which match the frequency of the vibration we are emitting. And our frequency changes as per our thoughts and feelings.

"Everything is energy, including your thoughts and emotions. Each message that you think and say with emotion, carries a specific vibrational energy that you send out in the universe."

• *Bob Proctor*

Thoughts and Emotions

Thoughts become things

I can't begin this chapter without the mention of the book *"Think and Grow Rich"*. Before the popularity and wild success of Rhonda Byrne's book, *"The Secret"*, which made the Law of attraction a popular phrase worldwide, it was Napoleon Hill who published the self-help books in 1937 – *"The Laws of Success"*, which he later condensed into *Think and Grow Rich* at request of American steel magnate and philosopher, Andrew Carnegie. Carnegie thought it would be worthwhile to teach ordinary people how to become successful by using power of thought, imagination, and inspired action. He thought that this could be done by putting together his own success strategies along with those of many other highly successful men in a book aimed at the common man. He asked Hill whether he would be willing to spend 20 years writing this book. Hill eagerly said yes, and the result was *"Think and Grow Rich"* who, as per the many claims made several people millionaires and billionaires who followed the ideas mentioned in this book.

"The starting point of all achievement is DESIRE. Keep this constantly in mind. Weak desire brings weak results, just as a small fire makes a small amount of heat."

* *Napoleon Hill*

Hill interviewed most successful entrepreneurs for twenty years and found out that there is only one success formula: a constructive thought with unwavering belief. He concluded that all the creative inventors and entrepreneurs used thoughts and vivid imaginations as a magnet to success. All these inventors might have differed on any other topic, but they agreed to this one thing, that "We become what we think!".

"Set your mind on a definite goal and observe how quickly the world stands aside to let you pass."

* *Napoleon Hill*

If you watch your mind closely, you will realize that you are continuously thinking all the time, and most of the time these thoughts are repeating in nature and not so positive. All suffering is because you do not know which way to think and what to do. But you have hardly witnessed your thought and without the necessary awareness of its impact on your well-being you are constantly suffering, all suffering that human beings are going through is just in their thoughts, in their uncontrollable imagination. A human being needs a certain level of psychological, emotional, and physical space, and a certain atmosphere for him to be nurtured. But a small negative thought can start a stream of negative thoughts and such a momentum gets generated that it looks impossible to come out from that psychological state if you have not caught that first negative thought early.

"If you have witnessed it, you know there is no other suffering like mental illness because the human mind has enormous capabilities. If these capabilities work in your favour, life becomes fantastic. If they work against you, there is no escape because the stimulus for suffering is not even coming from outside."

* *Sadhguru Jaggi Vasudev*

"If your hate could be turned into electricity, it would light up the whole world."

- *Nikola Tesla*

But the good news is, like any other skill - as you can learn to drive a car or play a guitar, you can also learn how to think constructively, which we will discuss in chapters ahead.

Now let's also discuss what a thought is and how it originates. Thoughts are the electrical impulses in the brain which are experienced by us in the form of images or words. They have different forms like reasoning, visualizing, judging, idea generation, problem solving etc. As everything is energy, thought is also a form of energy which travels at a very high rate of vibration. And if a thought is infused with a powerful emotion, it vibrates at an even higher rate and becomes very powerful.

They are best used when we think constructive thoughts deliberately to create our future, instead of thinking by default, which we do most of the time. Experts estimate that the mind thinks between 60,000 to 80,000 thoughts a day and most of them are limiting thoughts and not so positive in nature.

"I have a huge guarantee for you! If you don't make a decision and change your thinking, emotions, and habits in the next 6-12 months – You will achieve the same results and be in the exact same place (or worse off) than you are 2-5 years from now. You are either in a creation mode or destruction mode –

In our universe, nothing stays the same."

• *John Assaraf*

"Be very careful what you say to yourself because someone very important is listening...You."

• *John Assaraf*

Now I understand you are eager to go to the heart of this book, which has a complete explanation of The Law of Attraction, and you don't have to wait for long now. But even before that I guess we understood that thought becomes a thing. The reason I have kept this chapter before our next chapter is to only help you understand that only through the wonderful power of thoughts and emotions, you can manifest your desires using the Law of Attraction. Everything that you see around as a creation, it was a thought (idea) first. Before converting into a physical reality, it was just a vibrational concept which was thought upon long enough, that by The Law of Attraction the necessary momentum has been created around it to manifest it into a reality. So, any kind of repeated thought whether it's a constructive one or a destructive one will become a thing that means it will manifest in your physical world.

So, it becomes important that we articulate thoughts and ideas in a way that our brain can clearly understand what we want to manifest. Thoughts are the building blocks of what you want to manifest. So rather than a general thought that "I want to become rich" or "I want to lose weight", you must become specific about it so that your brain can act on it and implement it. Brain becomes much more cooperative with specific intentions and thoughts.

Abraham Hicks in their book "Ask and it is given" talks about the "17 second rule to manifest anything". As per them if you focus totally on something for 17 seconds, a matching vibration is activated, and now if you keep focusing then this vibration will keep getting stronger and the Law of attraction will bring you more thoughts that match. And if you manage to stay purely focused upon a thought for as little as 68 seconds, the vibration is powerful enough to begin the manifestation process. When you repeatedly practice focusing on a thought for as little as 68 seconds, then that becomes your dominant thought, and you will experience a matching manifestation until you change your thought process.

Emotions are the indicator of your current vibrational state

Emotions are the most intense experience that you always keep having. Emotions generate from the thoughts that you are thinking, so they are the direct indicator of what you are thinking. They tell if you are thinking constructive or destructive thoughts, they tell you in what kind of vibrational state you are in. That also means that at any given moment they indicate if you are heading towards manifestation of your desire or away from it!

"The emotions are this incredible gift that we have, to let us know what we're attracting."

• *Bob Doyle*

Emotions can go beyond the logical mind. It allows you to believe that you have the capability to achieve your wildest goals. Positive emotion is the tool used by the people of faith, people who are not sceptical about everything in life. Emotions become powerful forces of attraction as they have very strong vibrations. A thought is the engine, but fuel is emotion. Without emotion, the thought is just dry and will not convert into a thing (physical manifestation).

It's like with a pointed thought, you have put your engine (that will take you towards your desire) in the right direction, but it will not move until you infuse your thought with powerful positive emotions like hopefulness, optimism, passion, excitement, and joy.

That's why it becomes important that you remain mindful of your emotions. It's a wonderful dimension if you know the art of generating pleasant emotions. Once they are pleasant, they are not a problem to you and you will be inspired with a longing to go beyond your physical limitations, otherwise you will just keep trying to survive, fighting negative emotions, and not knowing your true potential.

"I will eliminate hatred, envy, jealousy, selfishness, and cynicism, by developing love for all humanity, because I know that a negative attitude toward others can never bring me success. I will cause others to believe in me, because I will believe in them, and in myself."

- *Napoleon Hill*

"If a steaming hot potato fell in your hands, you would get it off you as soon as you could. Do the same with negative destructive thoughts – just release them as fast as you can."

• *John Assaraf*

But even a negative emotion can help you remind of what you desire and what makes you incomplete. So, catching negative emotions early (so that they don't gather much momentum), and to learn how to use any kind of emotion creatively is important.

So, to conclude this chapter, learn to observe your emotions periodically each day, as they are our internal GPS telling us if we are moving close or away from our goals and desires. When you feel negative emotions like hopelessness, anger, sadness etc. then it's an indicator that you should immediately switch gears, think a more uplifting thought, change the topic of discussion, start breathing deeply or the best thing to do is to meditate. Do whatever makes you joyful which is the highest possible positive emotion. The Law of attraction says, "Like attracts like", "That which is like unto itself is drawn". So, when you purposefully think positive thoughts which in turn generate positive emotions within you, then the universe starts sending more positive thoughts to you which leads to a continuous state of feeling positive emotions.

"Deliberately guiding your thoughts is the key to a joyful life, but a desire to feel joy is the best plan of all. Because in the reaching for joy, you find the thoughts that attract the wonderful life you desire."

- *Esther Hicks*

Emotional guidance scale

Abraham Hicks in their most popular book "Ask and it is Given" has come up with a series of emotions, with an emotional guidance scale, that will help you work from feeling bad to feeling better about whatever you are experiencing at any given moment. If you find where you are emotionally on the scale and then try to find thoughts that feel just a bit better about it, and then you can take small baby steps towards Joy.

The Emotional Guidance Scale:
1. Joy / Appreciation / Empowered / Freedom / Love
2. Passion
3. Enthusiasm/Eagerness/Happiness
4. Positive Expectation/Belief
5. Optimism
6. Hopefulness
7. Satisfaction – Contentment
8. Boredom
9. Pessimism
10. Frustration/Irritation/Impatience
11. Overwhelmed
12. Disappointment
13. Doubt

14. Worry
15. Blame
16. Discouragement
17. Anger
18. Revenge
19. Hatred/Rage
20. Jealousy
21. Insecurity/Guilt/Unworthiness
22. Fear/Grief/Depression/Despair/Powerlessness

Abraham Hicks says it is impossible to jump to joy if you are in a state of feeling jealous, angry, or discouraged. So, give yourself time as you climb upwards and allow yourself to feel every emotion as you move. If you force the feeling of joy, it will feel inauthentic and false, and you will not be able to truly move and will fall back.

Move up the scale at your own pace. For example, when you are in a state of grief or depression (number 22 on the emotional scale), getting angry (number 17) might not feel like the most ideal way forward but it's actually a huge improvement in regard to your vibration. By allowing yourself to get angry you have already climbed several steps and improved your vibration. Keep doing this until you can feel joy, the highest creative energy. And in the joyful state you will be heading fast towards manifestation of your desires.

Why It's Important to Catch Negative Emotions Early?

So now you understand the emotional guidance scale, but still its best to catch negative emotions early. Have you ever gotten angry or anxious and then and then stopped for a moment and thought "what was I thinking?"

You haven't. That's the problem. Once intense emotions are in full effect, your conscious mind becomes powerless, and you don't remain mindful. The momentum is too strong for you to think your way out of it. It's not because there is something wrong with you, it's because this is how your brain works. Let me talk about a little science here, the part of our brain called the Limbic System is primarily responsible for your emotions. Now amygdalae are that part of the brain which is responsible for feelings of anxiety and fear. When this part of the brain is activated because of an intense, stressful experience, your brain will simultaneously turn off another part of the brain—the prefrontal cortex—which helps us to reason and think critically. Therefore, it's so important to catch negative emotions EARLY, before they become outside of your control.

So, it's important to recognize your triggers. What changes do you notice within yourself when you are having a particular negative emotion? You may want to ask yourself these questions for each negative emotion you tend to experience, such as anger, anxiety, fear, sadness, etc. How do you change physically? Do you change the way you stand or the way you breathe? How does your thought process change?

So, to reactivate the prefrontal cortex, what can you do? Put your hand over your heart, take deep breaths and focus on your breathing for 2 minutes. This synchronizes the heart with the brain and reactivates the prefrontal cortex.

CHAPTER THREE

The Law of Attraction is the secret sauce

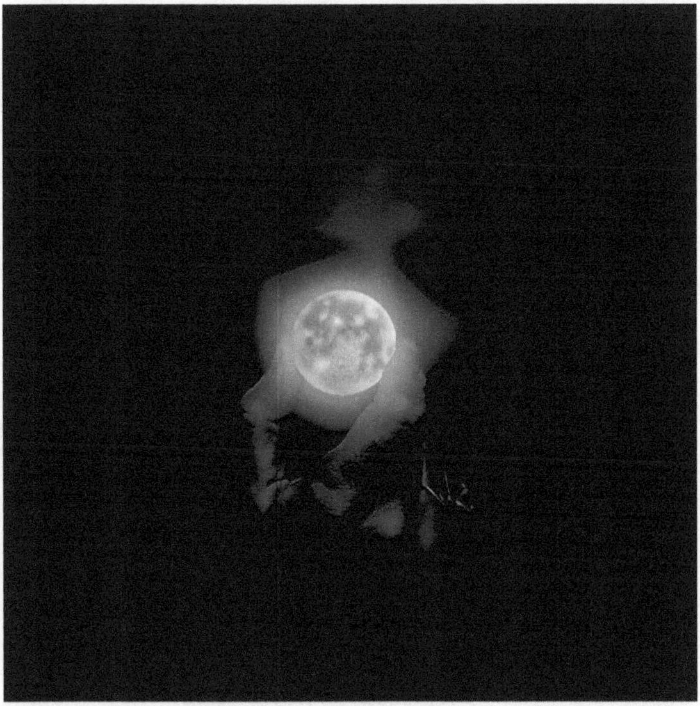

As I am sitting in my air-conditioned room on a lounge chair, sipping my tea and starting to write this chapter, from my window I am seeing hundreds of labourers including men and women working in the sun for wages as low as 350 Indian rupees per day. This reminds me of the question by many of my students that if manifesting money is easy then why there is so much of poverty in India or in the world.

What I always try to explain to them is that this is because most of the people are carrying the limiting beliefs about worthiness of getting abundance. They don't know what manifestation is, let alone the concepts behind manifestation.

"The Law of Attraction is always working, whether you believe it or understand it or not."

- *Bob Proctor*

And if you don't know the power of your thoughts, you are going to entertain negative thoughts also, that manifest the opposite of what you want. And as most people don't know that their thoughts have any power, so they don't remain mindful of their thought process and don't take on any practices to change their thought-style and remain exactly where they are.

For a long time, the ways of acquiring wealth and abundance in any area of your life, never came out in the public from the specialized circles of knowledge. People kept on believing that they can only progress this far, that their destinies were in the hands of others. Everything as it seems is the luck of the draw. Most of the people still believe that you must systematically and gradually move from one step to another to get success in any area of life and it is clearly reflected in how they function in their life. The parents, teachers and this society has succeeded in convincing you that you must really work hard, get higher grades, and go the extra mile to get the success. But as you will try to see the bigger picture, you will realize that though they want good for you, but these principles have even not brought real success to them. And then you will notice those who are getting success in every area of life with very little effort. Where your expensive education has not paid off that well, college dropouts are becoming multi-millionaires and billionaires. "Success is a gradual progress" is the biggest misconception. Ordinary routes may seem familiar, easier, and safer if you have a limited perception and you are unaware of the universal energies working with you. Once your thoughts, emotions and energies are aligned you can call on universal forces and can take the quantum leap. Isn't it provocative and exciting to know! But it will get even better as you keep turning the pages of this book slowly, taking deep breaths in between and meditating on each sentence you read.

I came to this realization shortly after I have started teaching this amazing law and the manifestation exercises, that a very small percentage of the population knew about it, so I made it my mission to collect all related information from all possible sources, understand it in more depth with an open mind, practice it for long and then distribute it to as many people as possible through all possible mediums, because it truly is life-changing. In no other time in history has mankind been able to access so much information via the internet. You literally can go on YouTube or Google, educate yourself on great insights, apply in your life and become abundant in every area of life beyond your imagination. Millionaires are being made every day, amazing relationships are being formed and perfect health is manifested, and the expansion won't stop as long as our imagination continues to expand. This book will help you to provide organized information in right chronological order and right tools with prerequisites mentioned, to get a life that you always wanted.

In this chapter I will give you the formula to apply in your life so that you don't have to settle for the things as they are now. Things will change dramatically for you if you read this chapter and the techniques discussed in upcoming chapters with full attention, with an open, unprejudiced mind and in a totally relaxed state. Life is now ready to give you a breakthrough experience. Furthermore, this formula requires far less effort than you have given in the past. This is the first time you will be coming close to your full potential.

What is the Law of Attraction?

The Law of attraction states that you will attract in your life whatever you focus on. You attract as per your dominant thoughts. The Law of Attraction is the most powerful law in the universe. It is always working just like Gravity. Now as we have discussed thoughts, emotions, energy and "who we are" in much detail in previous chapters, so it will be easier for you to understand this amazing law. We have discussed that everything is energy including us. We are a vibrational being and the extension of the source energy, of that Infinite intelligence that has created worlds.

"If you bring your mind to a certain level of organization, your body, emotions, and the fundamental life energies get organized in that direction. Once all these four dimensions of you are organized in one direction anything that you wish happens without even lifting a finger. It would help to assist it with activity, but even without doing any activity you can still manifest what you want, if you organize these four dimensions in one direction and keep it unwavering in that direction for a certain period of time."

- *Sadhguru Jaggi Vasudev*

"Whatever the mind can conceive and believe, it can achieve."

- *Napoleon Hill*

Your mind is like a powerful vibrational transmitter station that keeps sending signals in the universe as per the thoughts you think. Every signal has a different frequency based on the kind of thought (constructive or destructive) you are thinking. These signals are immediately received, understood and a matching signal is sent back to you by the universe. And thus, what you are offering at any moment in the form of thoughts and signals is changing your physical reality. Thus, you yourself are the creator of your destiny and are always in the state of creation.

"You are the one who calls the Law of Attraction into action, and you do it through your thoughts."

• *Rhonda Byrne*

"Thoughts become things. If you see it in your mind, you will hold it in your hands."

• *Bob Proctor*

As per the Law of Attraction, like attracts like if you are having thoughts that make you feel excited, appreciative, and joyful then you are emitting positive energy and you will attract positive people, events and circumstances in your life. Similarly, if you are having negative thoughts that make you feel sad, angry or resentful, you are emitting negative energy and you shouldn't be surprised by the negative results in your physical reality.

"If you want to find the secrets of the universe, think in terms of energy, frequency and vibration."

• *Nikola Tesla*

Based on the vibration and frequency you are emitting while sending energy through your thoughts and emotions you are attracting the similar energy back in the form of physical manifestations. So, you need to be mindful that your thoughts, emotions, and energy are linked with your desires, with what you want to attract and experience in your life. You must find the ways to hold yourself consistently in the vibrational harmony of your desires in order to manifest what you really want.

"Here's the problem. Most people are thinking about what they don't want, and they're wondering why it shows up over and over again."

- *John Assaraf*

We discussed that you think thousands of thoughts daily, which makes it almost impossible for you to tell if you are moving towards the direction of your goals and desires or away from it. We also discussed that your emotions are the indicator of your thoughts and tells you immediately if you are thinking constructive or destructive thoughts. The important point to understand here is, the longer you think a negative thought, the more momentum it gathers and as per the Law of Attraction you start receiving more negative thoughts and you start moving downwards further on the emotional scale. And thus, it will take more time to move up on the positive side of the emotional scale.

So be mindful of your emotions always, to know what kind of thoughts you are thinking and how its making you feel. This will tell you if your energy frequencies are in tune with what you want to attract in life. The earlier you catch a negative emotion, the easier it will be for you to pivot on the positive side of the emotional scale.

"Everything we as human beings have created on this planet first found expression in the mind, then it got manifested in the outside world. The wonderful things that we have done on this planet and the horrible things that we have done on this planet

both have come from the human mind. If we are concerned as to what we create in this world, it is extremely important that first we learn to create the right things in our mind. If we do not have the power to keep our minds the way we want, what we create in the world is also going to be very accidental and haphazard."

• *Sadhguru Jaggi Vasudev*

Now in case you have experienced something that made you feel terrible or depressed and thus negative thoughts and feelings have already gathered much momentum within you by the time you realized it, then also it's nothing to worry much. The moment you become aware that you are in loop of this negative thought process, make it your dominant intention to come out of it. While it's not easier to immediately jump out of it and it will be hard to gain access to positive thoughts, but any thought that gives slightest relief will be of much value. As per Abraham Hicks, there is tremendous value when you are able to deliberately cause even the slightest improvement in the way you feel. It means you may have regained some control on your thought process. Even though you are still on the negative side of the emotional scale, but now it's relatively easier to move back to the positive side on the emotional scale. And staying on the positive side on the scale will mean that vibrational matches to your dreams and desires will start showing up there and in no time, they will manifest in your physical world.

"Our job as humans is to hold on to the thoughts of what we want, make it absolutely clear in our minds what we want, and from that we start to invoke one of the greatest laws in

the universe, and that's the Law of Attraction. You become what you think about most, but you also attract what you think about most."

• *John Assaraf*

The Law of Attraction is not working

Many people come to me complaining that, the Law of Attraction is not working for them. I then explain to them that it's a Law so, it's always working! What they should ask is why it's not working towards manifesting what they want.

Below are the reasons for the same,

1. **You think more of what you don't want instead of what you want**

   Most of the times you never remain in the current moment, either you keep regretting the past or keep thinking the thoughts of the future that generate emotions like fear, hopelessness, or anxiety. And during these times you are continuously emitting negative energy, and you are offering a vibration that will attract experiences in your life that you don't desire. Or you may be thinking about your desires only, but with a doubt or disbelief that will they come true? Or whether you are worthy of it or not? And thus, without realizing you are still offering a negative vibration. And then you wonder why I am getting these life experiences as I always wished best for me.

Suppose you are set out to manifest a goal. No matter how difficult that goal may be to manifest, you need to visualize yourself as already being in that state of achievement. Suppose after a few days you start doubting yourself on whether you would be able to manifest such a goal, since it is very difficult. Here you are signalling a contradictory thought to your mind which goes against your desired manifestation process. And in a way you are telling Universe that though I love this thing but currently I feel I am not worthy of it, so I don't need it as of now till I come in a position to deserve it. And in such cases, you will not be able to manifest it.

"The law of attraction doesn't care whether you perceive something to be good or bad, or whether you don't want it or whether you do want it. It's responding to your thoughts."

- *Bob Doyle*

Let me take an example, suppose there is a man who wants to wake up early in the morning because he must attend a very important meeting at the office and meet the investors, who want to invest in his new business. But while going to sleep instead of thinking I should wake up early, he thinks I shouldn't be late for the meeting. Thinking in this way, what happens is, even going to bed early, he has a fear of getting late to office. And your mind thinks in pictures, so he starts visualizing the scenarios like missing the meeting or turning up their late to see unhappy faces of investors. Now what happens as per the Law of Attraction, the next morning alarm may doesn't work, or he gets a lot of traffic than usual while going to the office and finally he does gets late. This is the actual problem with most of the people, they always think from a bad side or from a negative perspective. For example, instead of thinking they want to grow rich, they think they don't want to be poor. Instead of thinking they want a good partner, they think hope I don't get a bad partner, etc. And what happens is, their fear becomes their reality, as they have put themselves in a bad vibration.

"You're getting exactly what you're feeling about, not so much what you're thinking about."

* *Bob Doyle*

When you practice The Law of Attraction in your life, always ensure that you are positive, patient, relaxed and vibrating at a higher frequency. Feelings of fear, worry, anxiety, desperation, and other low vibratory thoughts create limiting beliefs. Such emotions would inhibit you from achieving what you desire.

Practices like meditation and deep breathing, balance your mind and body. It activates the free flow of positive energy into your body and removes all blocks and negative energy from your body. This helps you to align yourself with the energies of the universe and thereby achieve your desired objectives very quickly.

2) Not taking inspired action

Another mistake that practitioners of this law do is, they don't take the inspired action as per the guidance of their intuition. When you progress with the Law of Attraction daily, you may notice that the universe starts providing you with enough opportunities to move ahead and achieve the desired state. If you don't take quick initiative during that time and grab the available opportunities coming to you then the results of The Law of Attraction could get delayed.

3) Intentions aren't clear

To attract anything into your life using the Law of Attraction, you must have a very clear intention that focuses on what you want. Your goals should be well thought of and specific, they should not be some vague ideas. If your intentions and goals aren't clear and they are weak, then will not be clear to the universe. You must know exactly what it is that you want, including details about your desire. Whatever you want, sit down, meditate, and take time to visualize exactly how it would feel in your life when you get it. Get clear on that feeling and have an intention for it to come into your life.

Your intentions should be as detailed and clear as possible. It may take some time to think about what you want, but it will be worth it in the end when your intentions are clear, and you start seeing results more quickly.

4) Lack of Gratitude

When applying the Law of Attraction, people tend to want more, and although that's fine, they often forget about being grateful for what they already have.

Appreciation is critical if you want to manifest things into your life because you must be grateful for it before receiving even more. Be grateful for everything you already have in your life and not take anything for granted, and then start looking at how you can receive more. The universe cannot give you what you don't appreciate! It doesn't matter how much money or material objects someone has; if they do not appreciate them, then no more abundance can come to them.

Remember, what you focus on is what you will become, and having an abundance mind-set with the Law of Attraction will help you manifest your desires more easily. Begin today by being grateful for everything in your life that has brought you where you are right now and watch as new things start coming into your life quickly!

The art of letting go

Letting go and allowing is all about removing resistance. If the Law of Attraction is always working and always attracting to you the energy that matches your dominant vibration, then logic dictates that if what you want is not showing up then there must be a "block".

We all carry a lot of emotional baggage. The difference is that some people hang on to it. You need to release the memory of past bad experiences so that you can create the space for good in your life. You need to release whatever may be keeping you from a happy and hopeful life. You can write all your bad memories on a paper and when you are done with writing the "negative stuff", take that page out, go to the toilet, say "Thank you, I don't need you" and flush that piece of paper or simply burn it. If it was about memories related to bad relationships, while burning you can say "I release the energy of relationships that felt bad, one sided, abusive, controlling, demeaning, demanding, and humiliating. The energy of this relationship has done as much damage as I have allowed. Now with more awareness and in releasing this energy, I allow for a space where new experiences can come in with a new positive energy."

Letting go also means, once you believe that you have set the right intentions you let go of your desires. From this perception letting go is probably the one step in the whole process where most people fail. It's not easy. It is particularly difficult because it goes against the very nature of our desires, our thoughts and our habits. How can you "let go" and not care about something you care so much about? Letting go of your desires means that you know you are worthy of it, you deserve it and you have trust in the universe that it will fulfil your desires.

To come into the mind-set of releasing and to let go, you need to remove all the doubts and worry regarding getting abundance in your life. You can use techniques of meditation and affirmation here. Understand it in this way; if you have placed an order on Amazon, then you will be sure that you will receive it. Yes, it may be possible that either it comes a few days early or a few days late, but it will come for sure. You don't keep tracking the order every minute. This is the kind of trust which is needed when you place your order to the universe!

"Everything that we want is downstream... And you don't have even have to turn the boat and paddle downstream, just let go of the oars, the current will carry you."

- *Abraham Hicks*

When you absolutely trust in the Law of Attraction and know that what you desire will and must come to you, then letting go becomes easy.

Doubt your limits

If you have an idea backed by your gut feeling, just go for it. Gut feeling arises when your intuition gives you guidance. Start acting as if your success is guaranteed. You may have already spent years cluttering your mind with doubt and scepticism, but now with the knowledge of the Law of Attraction you know that you have the universal creative forces working with you. This is the time to use your full potential and to take the quantum leap and that too with much less effort and in less time. It's the time to challenge the limiting thoughts and beliefs that you have gathered since childhood. Drop all the doubts regarding your true potential which got deeply rooted in your subconscious mind due to repeated thinking of limiting thoughts.

"If you must doubt something, doubt your limits"

- *Price Pritchett*

Most of us are unaccustomed to look at ourselves as the vibrational beings, as the extension of the source energy that create worlds. And thus, it's hard to view our lives in terms of energy and vibration and it can be hard to experience our mind as the radio transmitter and receiver. Even if you are sceptical, try to calm your mind with practices like meditation and hear that subtle inner voice, that inner guidance of your soul that knows your true unlimited nature.

My intention is not to convince you about this Law, because it's subtle. It's not like the Law of Gravity where you can clearly see if you leave something, it goes down and thus you can be convinced easily. What I am saying is, right now just suspend any disbelief, and start doing meditation to know your true self and act with complete faith. I will discuss simple meditation practice in chapters to come, to give you a jump start. Then try to apply the Law of Attraction on small goals with less risk, till you automatically drop old ideas about your limits post seeing the amazing results.

Till then behave like you have total conviction.

And once you slowly start identifying yourself as a vibrational being and have applied this Law in any single area of your life, you will understand that your real limits are far beyond your imaginary mental boundaries. And then you will not limit your dreams to what you think you can have, but you will go for what you really want! You will become a deliberate creator, holding the key to go wherever you want from your current situation.

More gold has been mined from the brain than from earth

Let me tell you this story which is taken from Napoleon Hill's famous classic book, *"Think and Grow Rich"*. It's a golden illustration of this very subject. Hill mentioned that one of the most common causes of failure is the habit of quitting when one is overtaken by temporary defeat.

An uncle of R. U. Darby went west to dig Gold. He staked a claim and went to work with a pick and shovel. After weeks of labour, he found the golden ore. He needed machinery to bring the ore to the surface. He went back, arranged money for the needed machinery and came back to work in the mine. The first car of ore was mined, and the returns were huge. After a few more cars of that ore something happened! The vein of gold ore just disappeared! His team drilled on, desperately trying to pick up the vein again but to no avail. Finally, they decided to QUIT.

He sold the machinery to a junk man for a few hundred dollars and took the train back home. Some "junk" men are dumb, but not this one! He called in a mining engineer to look at the mine and do a little calculating. The engineer advised that the project had failed, because the previous owners were not familiar with "fault lines". His calculations showed that the vein would be found just three feet from where the Darby had stopped drilling! That is exactly where it was found! The "Junk" man took millions of dollars in ore from the mine, because he knew enough to seek expert counsel before giving up.

Most of the money which went into the machinery was

procured through the efforts of R. U. Darby, who was then a very young man. The money came from his relatives and neighbours, because of their faith in him. He paid back every dollar of it, although he spent years in doing so. Long afterward, Mr Darby recouped his loss many times over, when he made the discovery that desire can be transmuted into gold. The discovery came after he went into the business of selling life insurance.

Remembering that he lost a huge fortune, because he stopped just three feet from the gold, Darby profited by the experience in his chosen work, by the simple method of saying to himself, "I stopped three feet from gold, but I will never stop because men say 'no' when I ask them to buy insurance". Darby was one of a small group of fewer than fifty men who sold more than a million dollars in life insurance annually. He owed his success to the lesson he learned when he quit the gold mining business.

"Before success comes in any man's life, he is sure to meet with much temporary defeat, and, perhaps, some failure. When defeat overtakes a man, the easiest and most logical thing to do is to quit. That is exactly what the majority of men do. More than five hundred of the most successful men this country has ever known told me that their greatest success came just one step beyond the point at which defeat had overtaken them. Failure is a trickster with a keen sense of irony and cunning. It takes great delight in tripping one when success is almost within reach."

• Napoleon Hill

So now you understand you don't get lucky, you make your own luck! The people we call lucky or gifted, they just "let it happen" they know that this universe, this source energy adores you and wants your total well-being. These are your own limited thoughts that restrict you from receiving the gifts from the universe. But as you understand the true nature of your being and your hidden unexplored powers, then it's time to claim your well-being and let them materialize in your physical world. Don't just evaluate yourself as per the skills you have acquired over the years till now but look for the hidden unused potential within you which will help you to take the quantum leap.

You must come out of the cocoon and fly now as you have found your wings. But even with your wings you can end up crawling if you don't feel passion about life. So, fuel your heart with passion, feel strong emotions of how life will be when you deliberately create it just at your wish. Let the heart take charge and make the emotional move towards your burning desires. Everything else that's needed will come from inside of you. All the resources you need, all the money you require, the people, the perfect opportunity, everything will start unfolding and coming magnetically towards you once you open your heart to this universe and realize your true self. With the practices discussed in chapters ahead you will be able to listen to your inner council, to the sounds that no one else can hear.

"Our job as humans is to hold on to the thoughts of what we want, make it absolutely clear in our minds what we want, and from that we start to invoke one of the greatest laws in the universe, and that's the Law of Attraction. You become

what you think about most, but you also attract what you think about most."

• *John Assaraf*

"Everything you seek and everything you experience – everything – is inside you. If you want to change anything, you do it inside, not outside. The whole idea is total responsibility. There's no one to blame. It's all you."

• *Dr. Joe Vitale*

CHAPTER FOUR

Conscious and Subconscious mind

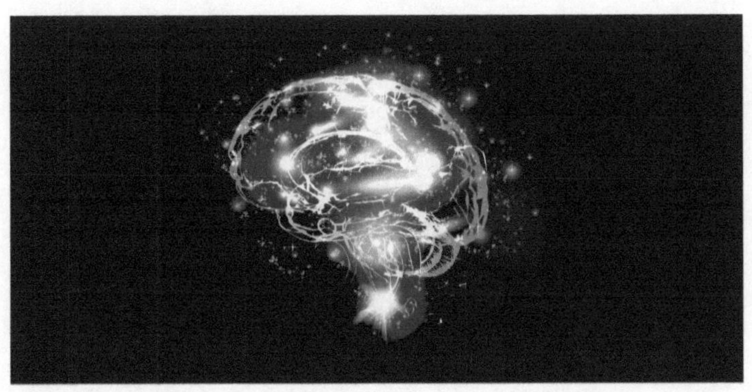

Mind versus brain

Mind is related to the brain. Most people do not find any difference between the two words mind and brain. Most people believe that the brain and the mind are one and cannot be separated. Most of the time these two words are used interchangeably. While the brain is a physical thing, the mind is considered to be mental. The debate on the difference between brain and mind has been going on since the time of Aristotle. Mind is considered as a pure vibrating energy, whereas the brain is considered a physical manifestation of the mind.

The Mind is like the equivalent of our computer software while the brain is like the computer hardware. The brain is the physical part of our organs in our body, while the mind is where all our information, feelings, emotions, and knowledge are being stored. As the brain is made up of several materials, it can be studied. On the other hand, it is hard to conduct studies on the mind as it is not made up of any material. Thus, people fail to understand the hidden and unexplored powers of the mind.

Now there are two levels of your mind - the conscious or the logical mind and subconscious or the emotional mind.

Conscious mind

Conscious mind is usually known as the logical, critical, analytical, or intellectual mind. Most of our decisions in our daily life are driven by our conscious mind. You think with your conscious mind, you accept or reject any idea using your conscious mind. In Sigmund Freud's psychoanalytic theory of personality, the conscious mind consists of everything inside of our awareness. This is the aspect of our mental processing that we can think and talk about in a rational way.

The conscious mind includes such things as the sensations, perceptions, memories, feelings, and fantasies. Things that the conscious mind wants to keep hidden from awareness are repressed into the subconscious mind. While we are unaware of these feelings, thoughts, urges, and emotions, Freud believed that the subconscious mind still has a strong influence on our behaviour. Freud often used the metaphor of an iceberg to describe the two major aspects of mind. The tip of the iceberg that extends above the water represents the conscious mind. While beneath the water is the much larger bulk of the iceberg, which represents the subconscious mind.

Subconscious mind

Subconscious mindis the place where all the information you gathered through your sensory organs and thoughts generated from realizations/emotions are stored.

While the conscious mind is important, Freud believed that it is far less vital than the subconscious mind. The things that are hidden from awareness and are lodged in the subconscious mind, Freud believed, exerted the greatest influence over our personalities and behaviours. You think with your conscious mind and whatever you think repeatedly, fuelled by strong emotions sinks in your subconscious mind and becomes your belief. Your beliefs (either positive or negative) are lodged in your subconscious mind. And belief is the energy that vibrates with one of the strongest frequencies and thus creates your life attractions. When you strongly believe in something, you literally create that into reality.

For example, if you tell a child, you are bad at academics and repeat these thoughts many times, it now becomes a belief. Even though the child has the potential to learn, he/she won't be able to create interest in learning because of the belief "I am bad at Academics".

Subconscious mind and the Law of Attraction

The subconscious mind and The Law of Attraction are closely linked because of the powerful frequency of a belief, which is only stored in a subconscious mind. You can't use the Law of Attraction without the subconscious mind being involved in the process.

"The subconscious mind is a fertile garden spot, in which weeds will grow in abundance, if seeds of a more desirable nature are not sewn therein".

• Napoleon Hill

Repeated thoughts can be considered as the seeds which are grown in the "garden" of the subconscious mind. So, choose thoughts carefully, because although they don't have much power by themselves, over time and with continued "feeding", they grow into ideas, beliefs, and attitudes.

So, consider thoughts as the seeds and subconscious mind as the garden. Knowing this automatically you will be careful of what kind of thoughts you are choosing. Though thoughts don't have much power by themselves, if deprived by emotions it will just be an empty and powerless thought, but if you think it continuously feeding it with strong emotions, it has the potential to sink into your subconscious mind, become your belief and thus manifest in your physical world.

"You must make certain to give your subconscious only suggestions, which heal, bless, elevate, and inspire you in all your ways. Remember that your subconscious mind cannot take a joke. It takes you at your word."

• *Joseph Murphy*

"Busy your mind with the concepts of harmony, health, peace, and good will, and wonders will happen in your life."

• *Joseph Murphy*

So, as you think thousands of thoughts daily and they are repeated in nature, thus you are continuously creating\ changing beliefs. If you are thinking fearful thoughts, you will draw your subconscious fears to you by the energy you give to them. Similarly, if you remain conscious of your thought process and feed thoughts related to your dreams, desires, and goals, you will then make positive beliefs and thus manifest these thoughts.

But if one moment you are thinking positive thoughts related to your desires and feel excited and the next moment you feel doubtful then you are sending mixed vibrations outside and the possibility that you will reach your goal will become remote.

"You might have heard of people who asked for something, and it came true for them beyond all expectations. Generally, this happens to people who are in faith. Let's say you want to build a house. If you start thinking, "Oh, I need 50 lakhs to build a house, but I have only 50 rupees in my pocket – not possible, not possible, not possible". The moment you think, "not possible," you are also thinking, "I do not want it. On one level you are creating a desire that you want something, on another level you are saying that you do not want it. In this conflict, it may not happen."

* *Sadhguru Jaggi Vasudev*

Limiting beliefs

Much of the programming or most of the beliefs that you have created are from childhood. When you were a child, you were presented with a lot of thoughts and ideas that were limited in nature like "Earning money is hard ", "Life is hard ", "There is too much competition outside". And your conscious mind was not able to filter these ideas as you were too young with limited perception of life and ideas of success. Thus, you absorbed these ideas of lack, limitation and struggle quickly.

Let me explain how such limiting beliefs affect us by discussing two examples.

Example 1

Shark experiment

You can't imagine a shark and other small fishes swimming together in the same large tank, right. But that has happened. A researcher brought a large tank, filled it with water and put a shark in it. As the first step of the experiment, he released a few small fishes into the same tank. The shark did the obvious; she attacked and ate all the small fishes.

Now the experiment moved on to the next step. The researcher placed a clear pane of glass in the tank separating it into two equal parts and dropped new small fishes into the other half of the tank. The shark rushed to attack the fishes but bumped off against the glass pane that it could not see. Frustrated with this she tried harder next time but to no avail. After many futile attempts in the next few days, she gave up.

Now as the third step of the experiment, the researcher went on to remove the glass and add small fishes, but the shark did not attack. Even when the barrier did not exist, the shark did not bother to attack. She has now created a strong limiting belief that she is unable to attack the small fishes.

Example 2

Elephant tied to a weak chain

You might have heard another story with a similar moral. A circus elephant tied to a weak chain does not attempt to break free even if the chain is as weak as a wafer. This is because as a baby, the old chain was good enough to contain the elephant. In its early days, it did try to break free but failed to succeed. Over the time, though the baby elephant grew into a huge mammal, the limiting belief in its head stopped any possible attempt.

Humans are no different from sharks or elephants. Most of the people do not achieve success as per their potential because they underestimate their own abilities. An animal may not be able to overcome limiting beliefs in its thoughts, but you certainly can.

Let me now give you my personal example.

My father came from a very poor farming family. Many times, he used to go barefoot to the school which was miles away. He belonged to a village which had handful houses and never even had electricity till a few years back. Only due to his hard work and good grades in education, he got selected in jail administration and reached till Jail Superintendent designation. And due to his hard work, honesty, and bravery in service, he got the most prestigious **"Presidential Gallantry Award"**.

It was obvious for him to think that success only comes from hard work and good education. He always kept saying to all his three children that education and good grades are of most importance to be a successful person due to immense competition outside in the world and we should work hard. I have been an average academic student but was good in arts and creativity which was of less value in the eyes of him.

Of course, he loved us the most and cared too much which was and still is so obvious to everyone due to his total commitment to his family. He always lead everyone by his example not just merely by his advices. He felt hard to express his love towards us, but his care and protection remains as a pillar of strength still in our lives. He loved to see all his family together and always took out time from his most demanding job to teach us, to take us around, to see that we as kids are not deprived of anything as he was in his childhood.

His expectations from his children were natural, but what was somehow missing (like in most of the families) was, to recognise the ability and interests of the children and let them perform on their own and to try to identify the signs that if child is over stressed and take an action immediately to soothe him and start a fresh to help blossoming the child naturally.

So eventually I developed these limiting beliefs in my subconscious mind that life is hard, I need to be good in academics. But these beliefs only made me feel inferior and my grades started dropping. Still somehow, I managed to get an engineering degree to become a software engineer which was always looking like a compromise with me, with my core self as I wanted to get into a field where I have full control to implement my creative ideas. One day, after spending 10 years in the technical area, I went to my manager and asked that I wanted to step up into a management role to use my interpersonal and communication skills better. But he told me that I don't have needed leadership experience and it will take me years to get into that place. That demotivated me a lot. Then one day I stumbled on an article about the Law of Attraction. I then read many books to understand it in depth. I followed suggested practices, felt alignment with my true self and within the next 3 months I got an opportunity out of the blue to manage a project in the same company for a leading luxury German Automobile client. I was leading a team of 50 people in the beginning which eventually expanded to 750 in the next 3 years. I never thought in my wildest dream to lead a team of this size.

Similarly, my brother also got into an engineering college, but left it after 3 years on the calling of his heart, to follow his passion - Animation. My father, mother and entire family supported him with his decision. Now he is one of the leading Animation artists in India.

"Passion is energy. Feel the power that comes from focusing on what excites you."

• *Oprah Winfrey*

How to help children overcome self-limiting beliefs?

Some children are shy, and some are not, while some children feel confident with interactions in public places or during activities and parties, others do not feel the same confidence. I personally use to hide behind the curtains or go under the bed, when unknown relatives or my parent's friends and their kids used to come at our home. Why his happens? What is the reason behind this?

The answer to this is simple: it relies on children's belief as to what they choose to think about themselves and their surroundings. Some examples of self-limiting beliefs that can prevent children from achieving their goals could be: "what if I cannot present myself well", "what if I answer them wrong?", "what if I'm not good enough in comparison to other kids?", "what if I sound stupid?", "what if I make fun of myself?" and the like.

To avoid children forming self-limiting beliefs or to change the belief system of children who have such beliefs, we must educate ourselves about the powerful effects of negative actions and words towards children.

I have a 9-year-old son currently, when I am writing this book in year 2022. Me and my wife always try to support him through critical positive reinforcement every day, for him to be confident, open-minded, and willing to take on any challenges without the slightest fear of failing and pressure of any comparison from anyone.

Saying things like; "I believe in you", "you are important to me", "we care for you", "we love you", "we are here to listen to you", "we trust you", "we know you can do this", "we know you can handle the situation" and so on, will guide the children to develop enabling beliefs that will lead to potential growth and success consequently. If you appreciate them, express gratitude, or speak about igniting their passion, you release positive energy and will start a circle of receiving favourable circumstances. Whatever you give, you receive.

As I practice meditation daily, so I understood early that meditation provides a unique possibility for every child to experience a joyful blossoming of their natural potential. But you can't force them to do that! It's a kind of voluntary thing, you only can influence your child or anyone to do it, if they see a certain dimension and love generating within you. You can carefully and gently guide your child to start this best practice available to any human being. Through an exploration of fun, love and joy, my son now enjoys doing different kinds of simple meditation practices with me daily. Meditation allows each child to develop and live in optimal health and inner peace.

"Don't burden others with your expectations. Understanding their limitations can inspire compassion instead of disappointment, ensuring beneficial and workable relationships. Remember that you have only a short time together."

* *Chagdud Tulku Rinpoche*

Receiving guidance from the subconscious mind

Whenever you are stuck in any problem or want to know the way ahead to achieve your goals, you can ask for guidance from your subconscious mind. So, the question is how? Below are the steps for technique to seek help from your subconscious mind.

- Find a quiet spot at your home where no one will disturb you for 20 or 30 minutes. Then quiet your mind by taking slow and deep breaths followed by 10 minutes of meditation while keeping your eyes closed.

- Keep your eyes closed and frame your question with clarity in your mind and be specific.

- Feel how excited and happy you will get when your problem will be solved, or you will get the direction towards your goal.

- Then you get busy with your daily tasks and let go of the problem from your mind and trust the answer will come soon and the process is underway.

- You will get an answer, at the right time. Call it gut feeling, call it intuition or instinct, or call it just revelation. Call it whatever you want! Just learn how to listen to those messages and to trust them! Because there is so much valuable information in them for your higher good.

The subconscious mind will always provide you with guidance if you trust it.

Mental and Physical healing

As the last topic in this chapter, I also want to discuss how the subconscious mind and medical treatments may work together to help your mind and body reach optimum health. If your dominant thoughts are negative, then they have direct impact on your health and almost on every other area of your life like relationships, career, and financial condition. You must understand that the problem is not with any outer situation but within you. You can use positive affirmations to reprogram your subconscious mind and to drop any limiting beliefs. Practicing affirmations will help you tapping into your higher self.

You can thus change the energy within yourself by releasing the energy of worry, fear, anger, and sadness and embrace positive energy by slowly moving towards more positive thoughts.

"Oftentimes your conscious mind interferes with the normal rhythm of the heart, lungs, and functioning of the stomach and intestines by worry, anxiety, fear, and depression. These patterns of thought interfere with the harmonious functioning of your subconscious mind. When mentally disturbed, the best procedure is to let go, relax, and still the wheels of your thought processes. Speak to your subconscious mind, telling it to take over in peace, harmony, and divine order. You will find that all the functions of your body will become normal again. Be sure to speak to your subconscious mind with authority and conviction, and it will conform to your command."

- *Joseph Murphy*

CHAPTER FIVE

Meditation and alignment with universal energy

Meditation

Meditation in the essence is being aware of all that is happening within you. Meditation provides you the best possible opportunity to become totally relaxed and totally aware of what kind of thoughts and emotions are getting generated within you. The modern world has become a restless world where we currently live. People are living in continuous conflict and tension in their minds. They feel huge pressure trying to live up to other's ideas of who they should be. This is the time to simply accept who you are and to realize your true self and true potential.

Through meditation and quiet contemplation, you can look inside and connect with your own deeper truth and wisdom and seek the most valuable counsel of your inner being.

"Meditation means dissolving the invisible walls that unawareness has built."

• *Sadhguru Jaggi Vasudeva*

"Meditation is the only way to freedom from stress, as it is a dimension beyond the mind. All the stress and struggle are of the mind."

• *Sadhguru Jaggi Vasudeva*

Realizing your true self to harness the power of the Law of Attraction

Abraham Hicks calls it the "state of allowing" which means you have quieted your mind and decreased any resistant thoughts. So that your vibration naturally arises, and you come closer to your inner being and get vibrationally aligned to your true self, with that infinite intelligence or source energy which is the Creator. And under such alignment you will thrive and attract your dreams and desires to you much faster.

"Your Inner Being, or Source Energy, always offers a perspective that is to your greatest advantage, and when your perspective matches that, then positive attraction is occurring."

- *Esther Hicks*

You cannot manifest anything from the place of negativity. When you feel negative emotions like sadness, anger, doubt, worry etc., if you attempt to use any manifestation tools like visualization or affirmation from this place it will be counterproductive. You will end up feeling more lack and thinking of limitations at that time which will take you further away from your desires and will manifest what you don't want. And eventually you may wrongly conclude that the Law of Attraction doesn't work! That's why calming the mind is the prerequisite before using any manifestation tools, which unfortunately many people don't understand.

Now you know "The Law of Attraction" is the secret to live an abundant and fulfilling life, but what is "the secret" to making the Law of Attraction work for you? Now the answer is obvious - Meditation. To manifest a fulfilling life, you must dissolve all your limiting beliefs and change your thoughts, which must be done from the root: the subconscious layers of your mind.

Meditation is the best practice that melts all the layers of negative emotions like worry, anxiety, depression, hopelessness, and fear etc. from your subconscious mind. Then with your crystal-clear thinking, you will be able to guide your thoughts gently towards your goals and desires and then manifestation of anything you want, whether it be love, good health, wealth or success in career will be effortless.

"Suffering is due to our disconnection with the inner soul. Meditation is establishing that connection."

- *Amit Ray*

Powerful CEOs, famous Hollywood actors, bestselling authors, well-known media personalities, top military rank officers, famous artists, professional athletes, and even billionaires say meditation is the secret to their success because it also enhances their intuitive capabilities. And intuition is your inner guidance.

Deep breathing technique

Breathing is one of the most important body functions, not only because we need to breathe to stay alive, but because it moves the energy in your body, releases resistance, and connects you with your true self, your inner being or that highest power.

Breathing is such a normal part of everyday life that it's probably something you don't think about often. However, the way you breathe can have an important impact on your physical and mental well-being. Deep breathing can help release chaos in your life and lines you up with the perfect picture that you see of your desires getting fulfilled and moves you a step forward towards manifesting it. While you are reading this try breathing slowly and deeply through your nose and see if you feel just a little bit better.

Below are the steps for the deep breathing technique:

- Find a comfortable and quiet place and sit with your back straight. You can sit in the cross-legged position on a bed or on the floor or you can even sit on a chair.

- Close your lips and inhale slowly but deeply through your nose for a count of six.

- Hold your breath for a count of five.

- Exhale slowly and completely through your mouth for a count of 6, making a whoosh sound.

- This completes one cycle. Repeat for five more cycles.

Simple meditation techniques

There are a wide range of meditation techniques available, but I am going to explain to you only a couple of them that I found easy and very effective, based on my personal experience. But remember to do the above mentioned deep breathing exercise always before doing any kind of meditation techniques mentioned below. This will help you to go deeper into the meditation and closer to your true inner self.

1. **Breath awareness**

Find a quiet place at your home and sit in a crossed leg position with palms facing upwards, placed on your thighs or on your knees. You could also be seated on a chair or on the floor on a cushion. Try to keep your back comfortably upright, and not too tight. Now do the deep breathing exercise and then close your eyes gently. Witness the emotions within you for some time and then notice the sensations in your body, the touch of clothes that you are wearing, the connection with the floor or the chair.

Keep a smiling face, this smile is coming from within and not forced. Now start noticing your breath. Feel the sensations in nostrils when you inhale or exhale. Notice coolness at the tip of your nose when you breathe in and warmness when you breathe out. Keep noticing for a few minutes. Now as you become aware of your breath, you become aware of your body as a whole, notice how your chest expands when you breathe in and how it contracts when you breathe out, keep observing for a few minutes. Now in between if any thought comes like, "what will I do, when this mediation practice ends" or "what's the other family members are doing right now" or any other thoughts, then don't worry, leave those thoughts there and don't follow any thought. Simply bring your awareness back to your breath. Any time your mind slips to any thought, bring your awareness back to your breath. Do this exercise for 15 minutes, then slowly open your eyes and stay in the awareness of the present moment for a few more minutes.

1. Third eye meditation

There is an energy centre, located in the centre of the forehead, known in biological terms as the pineal gland. It is also commonly referred to as the third eye. When it is activated, it enhances your intuitive capabilities.

To begin with this technique, choose your quiet location and then sit in a cross-legged position on the bed or yoga mat. If you are not used to sitting like this then for a few initial days you can sit on a chair or on a soft surface, like a pillow or a few stacked blankets. Do the deep breathing exercise for one minute. Then ensure your back is comfortably erect; your head upright and slightly tilted upwards, and then close your eyes gently. Place your palms facing upwards in your lap or on your knees. Now keep a gentle focus, between the eyebrows keeping your eyes closed and have awareness of your breath as well. Practice this meditation for 10-15 minutes. I personally do this meditation practice daily twice and feel deep relaxation and connection with my inner being!

"When meditation is mastered, the mind is unwavering like the flame of a candle in a windless place."

- *Bhagavad Gita*

Understanding mindfulness

Mindfulness is the quality of being aware of what we are, where we are and what we are doing. It keeps us aware of how we are responding to our surroundings and circumstances. Mindfulness is a quality while meditation is a practice to achieve this quality. Meditation is one of the many roads to a mindful living. Although meditation is highly effective for this purpose, it is just one of the ways to cultivate mindfulness. Let me discuss one example to make your whole day mindful and to keep your mind away from the obsessive thoughts.

Mindful walking

You may be already used to walk daily outdoors or indoors in the morning or in the evening, but you can do it mindfully now! While walking, walk at a natural pace and keep your hands wherever you feel comfortable - at sides or behind your back.

Pay attention to each step when you are lifting and dropping the foot. If in between something else captures your attention, bring your awareness back to the sensations of walking. If you are walking outside, you can also keep a wider awareness of the nature or of any kind of surroundings, without being judgmental about them, without labelling or naming them. Then after a few minutes you can bring your awareness to the sounds around, without getting caught up in whether they are pleasant or unpleasant.

Now when you will end your walk, just stay there for a few moments, and realize that you can spread this kind of awareness to any kind of task that you do, like you can take a bath mindfully. Notice when you place your hand on the knob, feeling the sensations of the water flowing down on your body, notice the change in temperature you are feeling and also notice the smell of the soap or shampoo. Similarly, you can do any activity like dressing, cooking, eating, brushing your teeth, or driving, with mindfulness. You can live your entire day with mindful intention. All it takes is attention, awareness, and the intention to be as mindful as possible while doing each activity.

"As soon as you honour the present moment, all unhappiness and struggle dissolve, and life begins to flow with joy and ease. When you act out the present-moment awareness, whatever you do becomes imbued with a sense of quality, care, and love - even the simplest action."

- *Eckhart Tolle, The Power of Now*

"Realize deeply that the present moment is all you have. Make the NOW the primary focus of your life."

- *Eckhart Tolle, The Power of Now*

Intuition and Inspired Action

Intuition (knowing beyond logic)

Intuition is something beyond your intellect; it is your soul's guidance, appearing naturally in a person during those instants when his mind is calm. When it is calm, then without distortion it can hear the valuable counsel of your Inner Voice. It also needs a certain faith to accept the counsel provided by your intuition as intuition is knowing beyond logic. If you don't have faith and think that anything that can't be supported by logic and explained by an intellectual mind cannot exist, then you will miss the opportunity to live in the higher realm of reality.

Logic versus intuition is one of the biggest battles within us. Your logic is based on the filters that are currently in place based on your childhood, societal programming, generational beliefs and thought processes. Intuition is based on your core truth, your true essence and doesn't get influenced by these filters. Over the time you get trained rationally and don't allow the higher self to speak to you, you end up denying it as a random feeling or imagination.

"I believe in intuitions and inspirations...I sometimes FEEL that I am right. I do not KNOW that I am."

• *Albert Einstein*

"Intuition is the highest form of intelligence, transcending all individual abilities and skills."

• *Sylvia Clare*

Leap of faith

Intuition is a jump, a leap of faith; it doesn't come to you step by step. Steve Jobs came to India during the 70s. He observed and concluded that people in India use intuitive faculty more, compared to any other place in the world. The reason was simple, Indians have always been the people of faith and less sceptical in nature. There is a close relation of faith and intuition. With faith you can transcend logic and develop intuitive abilities where things need to be grasped more than understood. Faith comes more naturally to some people while not to others. You need a calm mind, an open heart and simplicity to truly embrace faith. Faith makes the journey easy; you don't have to know how you are going to get there, you just need to know where you want to go.

"Don't try to comprehend with your mind. Your minds are very limited. Use your intuition."

* *Madeleine L'Engle*

"Intellect is not going to be your home. It is a small instrument, to be used only for passing from instinct to intuition. So only the person who uses his intellect to go beyond it can be called intelligent. Intuition is existential. Instinct is natural. Intellect is just groping in the dark. The faster you move beyond intellect, the better; intellect can be a barrier to those who think nothing is beyond it. Intellect can be a beautiful passage for those who understand that there is certainly something beyond it."

* *Osho*

To reach the destiny you don't need to have the perfect map, you don't need to have the perfect plan. Open your heart; understand the power of having faith and you will invite the sudden grace from the universal energy which always wants you to take a quantum leap! You don't need to wait to have everything organized and to remove all the risks before you make a move.

Realize that you have a source of power which is omnipotent - Intuition. But unfortunately, people have this wrong idea that an ordinary person can't experience it and it's accessible only to the mystics or highly spiritual people. But that's not true. Scientists, artists, and industrialists have been using it from ages to get success. Any ordinary person can access it through simple practices like meditation and mindful living.

For example, if you are an industrialist and have problems with a merger or acquisition or are a housewife having relationship issues with your husband, in laws or your children, then try this simple technique. Find a quiet place at your home, close your eyes, do two minutes deep breathing exercise. Then try to feel the inner being, the awareness of that source energy or God within you. Use your imagination to visualize something that will bring you closer to the source energy which you may refer as God. You can use something sensory that will focus your attention like music, flowing water, a flower, candle, image, or idol of him. This will take you in absolute peace and calmness and will soon bring you in alignment with source energy. Now prayer may be the best way to talk to God, the key to listening to God is in meditation. Then speak in the following, simple manner to that supreme power within -

"Dear God (or Universe), I know, you know all the things about me, and you love me. I am having this problem and I know you will provide me with the solution to this and give me the idea necessary". Now begin to imagine how it will feel once your problem is solved. Don't pretend but truly feel it. Then comes the most important part, "Let go of your intention". With full faith accept that you will receive the answer of your prayer and drop it. Slowly open your eyes, bow down and feel gratitude to that divine power and then get busy in your daily routine. Do not sit around waiting for the answer. It will come at the least expected moment. The inner voice of intuition speaks like a flash—it is always spontaneous and unannounced. You may get any type of information which will help you along the road to success. Intuition knows the answer and does not require previous experience. No reasoning power is involved and the amazing suddenness, with which the solution comes, sometimes is startling.

"Solve all your problems through meditation. Attune yourself to the active inner Guidance; the Divine Voice has the answer to every dilemma of life. Though man's ingenuity for getting himself into trouble appears to be endless, the Infinite Succour is no less resourceful."

• *Lahiri Mahasaya*

Inspired action

The Law of Attraction states that thoughts become things. What people sometimes miss is that intentions also need to be linked with actions. It still requires you to take action by acting upon the opportunities that come to you through the Law of Attraction.

You might have also heard this term repeatedly "Inspired Action". But what is the inspired action and how do you know when to take it?

Once the intention has been set and you try to remain constantly with your higher self, the universe responds by opening a sequence of doors to redirect your path.By following your intuition, your inner guidance system, you are gently nudged in the direction of these new opportunities. This new path will be the fastest, shortest and the most beautiful way to your desires. It always looks like an effortless action as you thoroughly enjoy it.

This inner guidance comes easily once you develop your intuition. It can come in any form, from ideas, to signs on the road, to comments overheard in passing a group of people, through any random social media post, through any particular page of a book you just opened.

But if you're stuck in your head overanalysing, rushing and being busy, you are never going to realize when the spirit is trying to get your attention. You must be present, open, and willing to receive the answers. Often you may ignore them, but it is the universe telling you to act now in a certain way, to receive what you have asked for. And when you follow them and act, you are taking the inspired action. As soon as your intention is in place, pay attention to the signs that can pop up anytime to lead you to your desires. For example, if you want to manifest a job, take note of surprising invitations that you may receive, and unusual chances to attend networking events. The universe may also begin to send you messages through people around you. You are having a conversation with a friend or family, and they suddenly say something like, "I bet you are going to the walk-in interview that's happening this weekend in this company". That's a sign!

When we feel inspired to do something, it's important that we take physical action while the inspiration is still within us!

How do you know if an action is truly inspired?

Here are some tips:

- Inspired action feels good. Ego-based action is based on fear (fear of losing and failure etc.).

- Inspired action is comfortable. Ego-based action occurs when you feel impatient.

- Inspired action comes to you unexpectedly. Ego-based action arises when trying to figure out desperately, how the things will happen.

- Inspired action comes from a place of allowing. Ego-based action is based on attachment to the outcome.

- Inspired action comes through practices like meditation, visualization, affirmation (which brings you in alignment with the universal energy) while ego-based action comes from the conscious mind.

Remember, if you want to fully harness the power of the Law of Attraction, you need to ask, believe, listen to your inner self, and take the inspired action. When you achieve your vibrational alignment and you feel inspiration to act, your action feels effortless. Any action taken without being into vibrational alignment with your true self, will not bring you desired results, will be a lot of hard work, inefficient and over the time will only demotivate you.

"One difference between successful people and all the rest is that successful people take action."

• *Bob Proctor*

"Action will sometimes be required, but if you're really doing it in line with what the Universe is trying to bring to you, it's going to feel joyous. You're going to feel so alive. Time will just stop. You could do it all day."

• *Bob Doyle*

Once you are in alignment with the universe, the Law of Attraction will provide you with all the resources, ideas, people, and money, which you need, to achieve your goals. But you should be in a state of awareness to recognize when the universe is trying to send these things and ideas to you. You should not dismiss them as mere coincidences. Everything you want is out there waiting for you to ask and then trust.

CHAPTER SEVEN

Setting up goals, desires, and intentions

Power of a burning desire

What is the starting point of the manifestation process and the Law of Attraction? ...It's "Desire ".

There is a popular real story in the book, "Think and grow rich" about Edwin C. Barnes who was very clear in his mind about "what he really wants". He was a very poor man at that time, but his dream was big. He had a burning desire to work with Thomas Edison and to become a business associate of this great inventor. Edison recalled his first meeting with him, when he was standing before him, looking like a tramp. Yet, there was something conveyed in his expression and manner, an extraordinary determination to succeed. That deep desire and intense resolve to succeed convinced Edison. He said, "Because of what I saw, I gave him the opportunity to stay around until he succeeded". And rest was history. When a person clearly knows what he wants and has a burning desire - not just a wish or hope, then universal energies are always working with such a person. Same happened with Barnes. At that time, the Edison lab had perfected a new office device, known as the Edison Dictation Machine. It had received only a poor reception and was about to be withdrawn from the production. But Barnes saw this as his chance. He approached Edison seeking permission to market this machine. He even had a slogan ready,

"Made by Edison and Installed by Barnes".

His proposal was accepted by Edison and Barnes had his long-awaited business partnership with him. It made him wealthy beyond anyone's expectation, by today's dollar's amount, almost 100 million dollars. Barnes had no money, had no specific skill, and had a very little education. But his clarity on what he really wanted made success a certainty for him.

It's a great illustration of the manifestation power if goals are very clear in mind and a burning desire is there in heart. It doesn't matter how big the goal is.

"Don't downgrade your dream just to fit your reality. Upgrade your conviction to match your destiny."

* *John Assaraf*

"Don't censor your dreams or vision with practicalities and probabilities."

* *Jack Canfield*

So as a first step of using the Law of Attraction, you must first set the right and specific goals, so that you can manifest your dreams. One of the most important things you can do to ensure you get what you want is at least to know what specific things you want. Doing something about it will be the second most important thing you can do. However, without an aim, you would have no idea what you want or how to get it. Many people fail to set goals at all, and those that do set goals, do so ineffectively and fail to review them at regular intervals. When it comes to manifesting with the Law of Attraction, this contradictory strategy may be the one aspect that can hold you back from manifestation. This could explain why you're having difficulty being one of those successful people who have it all. The Law of Attraction is one of the strongest forces in the universe, and when used correctly, it can completely change your life. You will become unstoppable when you combine it with a clear goal-setting formula. Without a clear goal how, the universe will know what you want, right.

"To create what you really care for, the first and foremost thing is that what you want must be well manifested in your mind. Is that what you really want? You must look at it, because for any number of things in your life you have thought, "This is it." The moment you reach there, you realize that it is not it – it is the next one and the next one. So, first of all you must explore what it is that you really want. Once that is clear and you are committed to creating it, now there is a continuous process of thought in that direction. Once you can maintain a steady stream of thought without changing direction, it will definitely manifest as a reality in your life."

* *Sadhguru Jaggi Vasudev*

Now while setting goals don't let the practicalities and possibilities mess up your aspirations or limit your dream. There is no dream of yours that you will be unable to achieve. If you can imagine it, you can make it a reality. You do not need to worry about every aspect of the journey. Focus on what you want; don't focus on how you will get it. "How" is the part of the universe to take care if your desire is deeply rooted in your subconscious mind.

If you think back to when you were a kid, you probably

remember having lots of wishes and desires. Even when you were young, you were encouraged to have big dreams for the future. However, when you entered adulthood, you started to get slightly different messages. Some still encourage you to make wishes, but a nagging voice in your head due to social conditioning starts telling you to be "realistic" about what you dream. This robs you from the chance to truly know yourself properly and achieve your wildest of dreams.

"If you must doubt something, doubt your limits."

• *Bob Proctor*

So, you now know that to use the Law of Attraction the first step is to ask. How the universe will help you if even you are not clear what you really want and what is your true potential. So, let's discuss how to identify your wishes, desires, and goals.

The best way is the traditional way of writing your goals on paper with a pen. I suggest at first, don't use a mobile or any electronic medium. Writing on paper forces you to think more clearly and hard about what you exactly want. When you are just thinking about your goals, you usually think of vague ideas, like to be happy or to be rich. But when you write it, you force yourself to be more specific about your goals, for example getting the soul mate of your dreams "what qualities of soul mate", the apartment of your dreams,"What will be the architecture of your home" or the work of your dreams, "what working hours suits you and what will be the working location" etc.

It also helps you commit. When you have written your goals down, you hold yourself accountable. That way, it will be less likely that you ignore them once you have put them down yourself on paper. For a better result make sure you write deadlines too. Holding yourself accountable against achieving them within a timeline, will get you closer and closer to your goals.

Writing your goals down yourself will give them a vivid image in your subconscious mind. You must unlimit yourself for thinking and dreaming big.

It gives you the chance to celebrate. You get to celebrate when you check off a goal from your list and reward yourself. Celebrate the small steps towards your goals too. This, in turn will bring more faith in the Law of Attraction and thus in dreaming big!

Abraham Hicks frequently uses below sentences in their rampage of appreciation. I want you to read them before you start writing your goals. While reading, feel the genuine emotions in your heart.

"Things are always working out for me.

Things are always working out for me.

Things are always working out for me.

Things are always working out for me.

Everything is working out for me.

Things are always working out for me.

And since I know that things are always working out for me, then what other things, I would like to define that I would like to be working out for me?

Since things are always working out for me. Then I want to begin to apply my attention toward more things that I would like to be working out for me.

I want to define more clearly what more things I want to be working out for me. What things?

Not general things, but what specific things would I like to be working out for me?

What things would really ring my bells? What kinds of things would really ring my bells?"

So, meditate for 10 minutes on these lines.Calm your mind and spend some quality time thinking of what you really want. To give yourself a head start, think of your ideal future and ideal self. Few examples of goals can be, "living in a beautiful landscape home", "running a company that positively affects thousands of people and brings you freedom and security", "finding the partner of your dreams", or "getting into that perfect shape and health". So, when you drop your limiting beliefs and then write your goals, they put you in a very optimistic frame of mind and provide you with the positively amplified feelings. This hopeful state stimulates the brain to begin searching for ways to reach your goals. That's where the subconscious mind's reprogramming begins. It may be hard for some to understand how large of an impact your subconscious mind has when it comes to setting our goals. Your limiting beliefs about yourself that are embedded deep in your subconscious mind, can generate thoughts and emotions of fear and doubt, causing you to lower your expectations and set your goals on a much lower scale. If you do not set your goals high enough, you will never reach your full potential. So, I want you to drop your limiting beliefs about yourself and then write your goals.

"Ask yourself what would you do even if you were never paid. That's a clue to what you should be doing and of course finding a way to be paid for it."

* *DR. Joe Vitale*

Last thing is to make goals measurable. Measurable goals are those that can be calculated. You may set specific goals, such as making a particular amount of money until a certain date or losing weight by a specific time. Measurable goals are essential because being clear and strategic about them, allows your subconscious mind to begin finding out how to accomplish them. Specific goals, with no vagueness or room for interpretation, are much more likely to be achieved than the general ones.

You can break your goals into 3 categories:

1. **Short-term Goals:** Goals that you want to achieve within 3 to 4 months.
2. **Mid-term Goals:** Goals that you want to achieve within 2 to 3 years.
3. **Long-term goals:** How you want your entire life to be in terms of health, wealth, relationship, and spirituality.

Now before you go ahead in reading further, it's your turn to get the pen and paper and start planning out for success! Sit at a place where no one disturbs you for next 30 minutes. Do the deep breathing exercise, meditate, and start writing goals in all three categories with timelines mentioned. Over next couple of weeks feel free to modify your goals as and when you gain more clarity.

Don't have a plan B

Taking againEdwin C. Barne's example, he never had a plan B. He burned all the bridges behind him and left himself no possible way of retreat. Hill in his book mentions that Barnes never said that "I will work there for a few months, and if I get no encouragement, I will quit and get a job somewhere else". He did say "I will start anywhere. I will do anything Edison tells me to do, but before I am through, I will be his associate". He had to win or perish!

"There is no plan B for passion"

*   *Chris Gardner*

Julius Caesar first became a champion of the people by leading the Roman military towards the conquest of great foreign lands. He advocated for reforms of an aging Senate and, fearing his uprising, they demanded that he relinquish his army. But Caesar refused and, instead, he marched straight to the heart of Rome. On the way, he had to cross the Rubicon River. No army had crossed the Rubicon with the intention to invade Rome in centuries. Caesar and his army still walked through the river. After he crossed, Cesar told his generals to burn the bridge down immediately.

There was no way out but forward. "Alea Jacta Est," he said — the dices are rolled. Rome would be the next stop.

Taking my own example - I was working in the world's leading multinational company 8 years back, which specialises in information technology services and consulting. I was living with my wife and one year old son in Mumbai. After a few months of job dissatisfaction due to the new role that I was forced to take, I decided to leave my high-paying job as I was not willing to compromise my freedom to take decisions. At the same time, I also wanted from long to get a job near my hometown, where my parents lived. Thus, without any other offer letter in my hand I resigned, which was very unusual during those times for a man with family! I didn't care that there are very few companies near my hometown. My well-wishers told me how "lucky" I am to have that job and to think again and take back the resignation. I thanked them for their concern but told that I am firm on my decision.

I had no Plan B! The day after I landed in my hometown,

I got a call from the biggest IT consulting Company in the world, which had its branch in Noida too (closest to my hometown). I was searching desperately for a job even in a small company near my hometown from past one year, but all my efforts went futile. But now I and my family were amazed on the timing of this opportunity. I went through the multiple rounds of the interview process smoothly and with a jet speed, as if someone was guiding me step by step. Finally, I was selected in no time and was offered a role and salary package way beyond my expectation in one of the nearest cities (Noida) located from my hometown (Agra) connected by a best world class express highway (Yamuna expressway) existing in India! Something was working with me miraculously - aligning the people, circumstances, and events into my favour because of my unwavering faith! And by that time, I never even have heard about this amazing Law of Attraction. But it didn't matter at that time because the faith, relaxation, and the alignment that I had felt with my inner being had ensured my absolute well-being.

Once I understood the Law of attraction later after few years, I learned the secret and the reason of the divine timing that I noticed. The reason was a negative feeling like desperation brings resistance whereas positive feelings, relaxation and faith bring a free flow movement towards your desires.

"There's no reason to have a plan B because it distracts from plan A."

- *Will Smith*

The first person who must believe in you has to be yourself and so there should be no such thing as plan B. Your plan A should be your plan B, plan C, and plan D. I realized that this is actually true, and this is what sets apart many of the successful people today. The moment you doubt if your original plan is going to work or not, you have already failed in a way. You will meet many people, your friends, colleagues, relatives who find themselves stuck in life and have a desire to move out, to pursue their dreams, but a little over thinking makes them conclude that "it's not meant to be" even before they took the first step or exhausted all efforts to fulfil it.

Many people simply follow what society tells them to do. They fear what other people will say and the negative results they can get for not bending to what society dictates. Just imagine how many more people like Steve Jobs, Elon Musk and Bill Gates would be there if people simply did not give up on their original plans. Sometimes, when we use our head, we tend to over analyse our situation. This makes us second guess ourselves and lose faith in what we can do. Remember your college days when in examination you look over the multiple-choice questions and automatically know the right answer based on your gut feeling. But after noticing the other options, you will get confused and change your answer which was not correct!

To conclude, we all have big dreams and want to take that unknown path towards them. Most of the time however, the idea that it will not work out prevents us from considering it or working hard towards it.

Thus, stop being realistic and start being optimistic!

CHAPTER EIGHT

Believe

Take the first step in faith

Now that we have discussed the goal setting formula in the previous chapter, and you may not know the exact path to achieve your goals, you must have faith now in the universe that it will unfold the path for you step by step.

There is one beautiful story that I have read, mentioned below.

There was a businessman who was sitting in a park looking anxious and very worried. He was in debt, a lot of debt. Suddenly an old man came towards him and asked the reason of his worry. With initial hesitation, he opened and said that suppliers are demanding long due payments from him, and he doesn't have any money, he is on the verge of bankruptcy. Hearing this old man sympathized with him and disclosed that he is none other than John Davison Rockefeller (an American business magnate and philanthropist). He wrote a check to him of half a million dollars and said, "Take this money. We will meet here exactly in one year, and you will be able to return it to me at that time". And after that he went away. The businessman was happily surprised, thinking he got the solution to all his worries. But strangely he decided not to use the check and he put it into his safe. The knowledge of the existence of his check has given him strength and optimism. He worked again and got such a success in a short time that without using the check he made a lot of profits and was able to clear his debts.

After exactly one year, he went back to the park with the same check and the old man also appeared. The moment the businessman picked out the check from his pocket, a nurse ran up and grabbed the old man. "I hope he wasn't bothering you. He always runs away from the house and tells the people that he is John Rockefeller", she said! The businessman was puzzled. During the whole year he was building a business, buying, and selling, convinced that he had half a million dollars with him. And suddenly he understood that it's not the money, real or imaginary, that turned his life up. It was his faith that gave him strength to achieve everything that he had now.

Once you have faith in your dreams truly, the Law of Attraction will take care of the rest and it will provide you with all the resources that you need, through ways outside of our normal understanding. The money, right people, ideas, opportunities, everything will come to you with the magical power of your belief. The Law of Attraction is always working. And now as you know it, it's time to claim abundance in every area of your life.

"Just take the first step in faith. You don't have to see the whole staircase. Just take the first step."

- *Martin Luther King Jr.*

I don't want you to believe everything I mentioned, in all the previous chapters at once. I just want you to take baby steps to explore them by yourself. Once you know by yourself through practices like meditation, visualization or affirmations, there will be no need to believe blindly.

If you read about information gathered based on my own experience and it appeals to you, but you don't just stay with the intellectual understanding. Instead, you try to find out by your own experience based on the tools I have discussed and will be discussing in next chapters, then it will be your first step in faith. You will see it from your own eyes. So, you don't cling to my words, but you experience it by yourself and move into this amazing mystical experience. Just reading my words will just be collecting information and you can say, "Yes, I know now much about the Law of Attraction now". But your knowing will be a deception.

By experiencing the methods, themselves that I teach in my Master class and workshops, several people across the world from different cultures and religions, keep sharing their story of how the revelation and personal experience of this amazing Law of Attraction has changed their lives. Your baby steps will help you to know who you truly are and how the Law of Attraction works. Then it will be easier for you to believe in the larger picture and then you can totally surrender to this universe to this amazing Law of Attraction. This unwavering faith in universal energies will then become your guiding light and guardian angels!

"I started studying successful people, a lot of successful people and the first thing they told me is you first have to believe it in here before you see it out here."

• *John Assaraf*

When your intention is powered by faith, it easily reaches to your subconscious mind and universal energy starts responding to it quickly due to the vibrational match you have now became to your desire by the power of faith.

"All thoughts which have been emotionalized and mixed with faith, begin immediately to translate themselves into their physical equivalent or counterpart"

* *Napoleon Hill*

You can create your misfortunes as easily as abundance, if you believe you are unworthy of your desires. This will create a negative thought impulse and will manifest poverty, ill health, or bad relationships in your life. But if you believe that you are the most fortunate man or woman on earth and act as if you already have what you desire, then this will be a wonderful example of faith and you will manifest it in no time!

"Faith and fear both demand you to believe in something you cannot see. You choose!"

* *Bob Proctor*

Begin with manifesting small desires to strengthen your faith

Let me give you an example of a real-life story of an Indian girl that I read on the secret.tv website of the well-known author Rhonda Byrne.

The Indian girl named Khushbu writes:

"I came across The Secret when I had seen one of my friend's

status. On it was posted "Thoughts Become Things". I got so curious to know what this phrase meant that I immediately checked on the internet and finally came to know about The Secret. Since then, I have been a strong believer of The Secret and I have manifested a lot of things.

The Secret says to start with something small that makes your belief strong. So, I started maintaining a journal and started believing that whatever I write in it will definitely manifest. I started with a cup of coffee, receiving Roses, free lunch, perfume, a compliment and much more.

Just a week back I had something on the checklist that I had written in this journal. It was an anklet that I had not manifested yet, but I knew that somehow it would come. I just needed to relax.

And guess what? Yesterday I received an anklet from my aunt that she bought for me from Hong Kong. I was so happy that I could not believe it.

Let go and 100% it will be yours. I always do 'small things' all the time just to strengthen my belief in LOA and to remember that anything is possible.

Ask and it will definitely be yours! Thank you! Thank you! Thank you so much, Universe."

If you are newly introduced to the Law of Attraction and yet to experience your manifestation power, then I will suggest you try manifesting small things first to strengthen your faith.

In my workshop when I work with my clients, I see often that they find it difficult initially to let go of the desires. But if you begin with smaller goals the benefit will be that you will be less attached to them and can easily let it go once placing your intentions. In this way you will be in allowing mode by showing trust towards the universe. And by and by it's inevitable that you will experience that you are not alone and once the universal energies are aligned with you, you can do the things you have never imagined as remotely possible.

So, begin with manifesting small things like a parking space, a cup of coffee, a text message or recognition at the workplace. Manifesting small things is a good way to practice letting go and allowing the universe to do for you what you cannot do for yourself. So, start small to build your trust in the universe. My first conscious manifestation was a particular spot in a busiest restaurant at a peak hour on a weekend, second was a text message.

Universe can't differentiate a desire as big or small. It works beyond the time, space, and size. To the universe there is absolutely no difference between manifesting 1 $ or 1 million $. The difference between these two exists only in your minds. Small things manifest easily because you easily come into the allowing mode as you have no resistance due to the fact that your life is not dependent on it, so you don't bother if it manifests or not. You can easily let it go.

"When people ask us how long does it take for something to manifest, we say, It takes as long as it takes you to release the RESISTANCE. Could be 30 years, could be 40 years, could be 50 years, could be a week. Could be tomorrow afternoon."

* *Esther Hicks*

The Abundance mind-set

The term "Abundance mind-set" originated from Stephen Covey's most popular book *"The 7 Habits of Highly Successful People"*. This book provides many useful ideas but let's discuss the concept of two types of mind-sets - abundance or scarcity of resources (time, money, etc.).

An abundance mind-set is the view that there is no competition with anyone and there are enough resources existing always for all to share. While the scarcity mind-set is an idea, that there is a shortage of resources in the world and high competition to get them.

"If someone is not receiving what they are asking for, it is not because there is a shortage of resources; it can only be that the person holding the desire is out of alignment with their own request. There is no shortage. There is no lack. There is no competition for resources. There is only the allowing or the disallowing of that which you are asking for"

* *Abraham Hicks*

Like most of us, since my childhood I heard my parents, relative and teachers repeatedly saying these phrases:

- Money doesn't grow on trees.
- Too much money is bad and doesn't bring happiness.
- There is too much competition outside.
- You are too thin and not growing fast.

They were obviously my well-wishers but were unaware of the effects of mind conditioning on the physical reality. It has caused constant feelings of anxiety and fear within me. I ended up growing thinking that I will never get success and don't deserve a good life as life is hard and I don't have the needed skills even to survive. I failed a lot in many aspects of life till I reached college and gained some level of confidence and self-alignment. If you are unaware of simple subconscious mind reprogramming techniques, it can be hard to undo a mind-set with which you have lived for a long time. But with the Law of Attraction tools and subconscious mind reprogramming techniques, you can melt all the layers of fear, worry and doubt and reprogram your subconscious mind completely with positive beliefs to get success in every area of your life.

"Never use the terms, "I can't afford it" or "I can't do this." Your subconscious mind takes you at your word and sees to it that you do not have the money or the ability to do what you want to do. Affirm, "I can do all things through the power of my subconscious mind."

- *Joseph Murphy*

Developing an abundance mind-set means being grateful for what you have and hopeful for what all you can achieve knowing your unlimited potential. This attitude automatically makes you happier and more creative. It improves all aspects of your life equally, from getting great opportunities at work to improving your relationships, health and finances and making you a more spiritually aware being.

"There is no virtue in poverty; the latter is a mental disease, and it should be abolished from the face of the earth. You are here to grow, expand, and unfold—spiritually, mentally, and materially. You have the inalienable right to fully develop and express yourself along all lines. You should surround yourself with beauty and luxury."

• *Joseph Murphy*

Finally, to help you achieve an abundance mind-set, don't compare yourself with anyone. Looking at the lives of others on social media etc., you can easily get into a scarcity mind-set by comparing your life to theirs. But this unhealthy comparison is a losing formula. You are seeing the best moments of a person on social media! Instead try developing genuine feelings of happiness for them and also look at what all you have got instead of what is missing. This will be your winning formula.

CHAPTER NINE

Visualization

In this chapter and the next 4 chapters, we will discuss the major 5 manifestation techniques one by one. Manifestation techniques are the practices or daily rituals which can help you achieve your desires. It's possible that your subconscious mind may try to resist these practices at first but persisting this with an open heart and mind is the key to successful manifestation.

Now coming to this chapter, many psychologists claim that 1 hour of visualization is worth 7 hours of physical effort! Visualization is one of the strongest tools in getting your dreams come true. It utilizes the faculty of your imagination and creates vivid life-like mental images of the desires you want to manifest. These visual images evoke strong positive feelings as if your desire has already manifested. Your subconscious mind understands images far better than it can understand words. Thus, this technique plants the seed of your desire very deep in your subconscious mind and replaces any limiting belief related to your desire with an empowered belief. It gets reprogrammed slowly and slowly and starts accepting these images as a reality. And then begins to shift universal unlimited resources in your favour. By and by the right opportunities, people, ideas, skills required, or any other kind of resources are sent your way by the infinite intelligence or universe, to help make our desire a reality.

Experiment conducted on power of visualization

Athletes participating in the Olympics work too hard for their events. Apart from the physical training they do the mental training too. Data has shown that athletes who visualize themselves crossing the finish line first are more likely to do it.

Russian scientists conducted an experiment on four groups of Olympic athletes. Each group had to do physical and mental exercises but in different ratio.

Group one: 100% physical training

Group two: 75% physical training & 25% mental training

Group three: 50% physical training & 50% mental training

Group four: 25% physical training & 75% mental training

The finding was that the fourth group performed best during the Olympics. Since then, the US Olympic committee has increased the number of psychologists to train their team.

As told to Forbes, according to Michael Phelps's coach Bob Bowman, who is U.S. Olympic men's swimming coach, "For months before a race Michael gets into a relaxed state. He mentally rehearses for two hours a day in the pool. He sees himself winning. He smells the air, tastes the water, hears the sounds, sees the clock". According to Bowman mental rehearsal is a proven, well-established technique to achieve peak performance in nearly every endeavour. "The brain cannot distinguish between something that's vividly imagined and something that's real". To manifest your dreams, it takes action, but to invoke an inspired action, which is the shortest and easiest path to your goal;

your subconscious mind should clearly know what you want and that you truly believe in it. And visualization is the perfect tool for that.

"Logic will get you from A to Z; imagination will get you everywhere."

• *Albert Einstein*

Do a small exercise now – once you read instructions, close your eyes and then only experiment.

Instruction:

Imagine slowly with our eyes closed that you are going towards your refrigerator. You have opened it now and picked up a lemon from the top shelf or wherever you generally keep it. Take your time to imagine and feel the coolness of lemon in your hands. Now imagine you have put it on the kitchen's slab and cut it in half with a knife. Now you are holding a half piece of lemon in your hand. Imagine you are squeezing that lemon in your mouth with its sour juice dripping on your tongue. Continue to imagine tasting its sour juice.

<u>*Now before reading further, do this experiment!*</u>

Ok now as you have done it! If you have imagined it correctly without any hurry, your mouth would have salivated and got watery. What has happened here? Your mind has tricked your body. The same is also true when you visualize your desires manifesting, your desires start coming to you. Brain scans have also shown that actually doing something and visualizing doing that same thing appears the same to the brain.

"Rather than being so ready to jump into action to get the things that you want, we say think them into being; see them, visualize them, and expect them—and they will be."

• *Esther Hicks*

The key to the visualization technique is to just visualize the end result, relax totally and enjoy. For example, the end result could be a great job offer that you are receiving from HR in the office or feeling happy while seeing the offer letter in your mail – *don't visualize the entire interview process.* The end result can be a relationship that you always wanted, see yourself holding hand of your partner and walking. It can also be a weight loss, see yourself standing exited on the weighing machine, showing the exact weight that you always wanted. Or see yourself holding the steering of the car that you always desired. Just visualize it in your mind and see yourself touching it and feel the emotions of having it in your life. One of the most important things about visualization technique is to just focus on the end result as I said, without worrying about how you will get it. Because the best thing about the Law of Attraction is, your part is just to declare what you want and by when. And when you enjoy visualizing the end result, it raises your vibration up to your desires. So just think about what you want and "how you will get it", let the universe take care of that.

"Imagination is your most powerful faculty. Imagine what is lovely and of a good report. You are what you imagine yourself to be. You avoid conflict between your conscious and subconscious in the sleepy state. Imagine the fulfilment of your desire over and over again prior to sleep. Sleep in peace and wake in joy."

*   *Joseph Murphy*

Right way to do a visualization practice

The Law of Attraction visualization is more than just using your mind to create a mental image of you realizing your goal. It is not just about thinking about your desires. It is not about the mind energy at all. The Law of Attraction visualization is about your heart and using heart energy to create. You see, when The Law of Attraction visualization is done correctly it's like a love affair. Be in the scene as if you are seeing through your eyes, hearing through your ears, touching through your hands or tasting through your mouth. You are not watching a picture from the outside. You are living the experience as if it is as real as you are now.

For example, if you have a desire *"to live in a beautiful house with your spouse and children on a hill station"*. Then to start this practice, first find a quiet place at your home where you will not be disturbed for another 20 minutes. Then sit in a crossed leg position with palms facing upwards placed on your thighs or on your knees. You could also be seated on a chair or on the floor on a cushion. Try to keep your back comfortably upright, and not too tight. Now close your eyes gently and do deep breathing exercise followed by breath watching meditation or third eye meditation for 8 to 10 minutes. You can also do any kind of other meditation practice that you are comfortable with.

Post meditation practice keep your eyes still closed and now move towards the visualization exercise. If you wish, you can now lie down on your bed with legs stretched or take any other comfortable position as you like, to do this exercise. Assume it's the winter season and imagine you are lying in a comfortable bed in the bedroom in your beautiful new dream house. Feel the bed sheets on your skin and the soft pillow under your head. Smell the detergent used to wash the bed sheets and pillow covers. Feel the gentle breeze coming in through the window as it drifts over your skin. Hear your partner breathing softly next to you. Then imagine getting up and sitting on the couch in front of the fireplace with a warm cup of hot chocolate or coffee in your hands. Feel the heat of the cup as you hold it. Hear the crackling sound of the woods on fire. Feel the heat coming off the fireplace. Bring the cup up to your nose and breathe in the delicious smell of the chocolate or coffee. As you take a sip, feel the chocolate hit your lips and tongue. Smile as you look over at your kids who are sitting at the other cosy corner of the room and are planning tomorrow's skiing or sight-seeing trip. Listen to them laugh and getting excited. Immerse yourself completely in the scene!

This is the real Law of Attraction visualization. You must go into details and feel it. Go beyond just having something. See how you would actually use it. See what it would allow you to do. Really experience the moment. Feel at one with the vision. Give it a lot of love. Enjoy it and really take it to the next level. Stay connected to it as much as you can and redo this as frequently as you can. Let the universe make it happen. You just enjoy the ride.

"Your imagination is your preview of life's coming attractions."

• *Albert Einstein*

Einstein already taught us the power of imagination and visualization that many others have written about in the last two decades. As per him - before we can make anything into a reality, we must imagine that it is possible. He even went so far as to say that "Imagination is more important than knowledge".

"Man's only limitation, within reason, lies in his development and use of his imagination."

• *Napoleon Hill*

According to Napoleon hill we are using the power of imagination in a very elementary way, but if we start using the imagination creatively, the finite mind of man can directly communicate with the infinite intelligence of universe (the faculty that sends hunches and inspirations to us).

All the great scientists, poets, musicians, artists, and industrialists became great by using this technique.

Story of Coca-Cola - The secret formula was IMAGINATION!

Napoleon Hill has mentioned a wonderful story of how Coca-Cola was made, in his legendary book *"Think and Grow Rich"*. He has mentioned about an old country doctor who goes to a town drug store and meets a young drug clerk. He shows him an old-fashioned kettle and a big wooden paddle (used for stirring the contents of the kettle). The clerk inspected the kettle and gave the doctor $500 (his entire savings). The doctor handed over a small slip of paper on which was written a secret formula to start the kettle to boiling. But neither the doctor nor the young clerk knew what fabulous fortunes were destined to flow from that kettle. The old doctor was happy getting 500 dollars for an old kettle, while the clerk was using his intuitive power and imagination. He was getting a feeling that it's not just a kettle but an IDEA and thus he took a big chance by staking his entire life's savings on this old kettle and a piece of paper!

The actual performance of that kettle began to take place after the clerk mixed with the secret instructions an ingredient of which the doctor knew nothing. Only due to this old kettle, different kinds of biggest industries were set up to provide sugar, refining, marketing, packaging of the final product, which was - Coca-Cola! This kettle and the idea generated in the clerk's mind made him rich beyond imagination and provided jobs to millions of the people. It had converted a small southern city into the business capital of the south, where it since then benefits, directly, or indirectly, every business and practically every resident of the city.

What an inspiring story it is!!

"Begin morning run," I said to Max. "Bifrost track." The virtual gym vanished. Now I was standing on a semi-transparent running track, a curved looping ribbon suspended in a starry nebula. Giant ringed planets and multi-coloured moons were suspended in space all around me. The running track stretched out ahead of me, rising, falling, and occasionally spiralling into a helix. An invisible barrier prevented me from accidentally running off the edge of the track and plummeting into the starry abyss. The Bifrost track was another stand-alone simulation, one of several hundred track designs stored on my console's hard drive."

- *Ernest Cline, Ready Player One*

Ideally, you should make creative visualization a daily part of your lifestyle.

Most people find it useful to set aside a specific time for the visualization, such as a fifteen-minutes period before going to sleep or after waking up. But the most important thing is that you maintain your ritual of visualizing your goal until you obtain what you want in your life.

"Visualize the most amazing life imaginable to you. Close your eyes and see it clearly. Then hold the vision for as long as you can. Now place the vision in God's hands and consider it done."

- Marianne Williamson

Create a detailed vision, feed emotions of excitement and joy to it and you will notice that your subconscious mind treats the image as a map to take you closer to manifesting what you have visualized clearly. Visualization is the most effective way to put the Law of Attraction into action.

Remember your childhood when you used to live in the present moment most of the time, with no regrets of the past and no worry for the future. You were living then in a pure vibration within you. Thus, automatically the skill like visualization comes to you naturally as you were not emitting the mixed vibrations. With your imagination you have turned a piece of paper into an aircraft, or a cardboard into a home. You have imagined and executed the weddings of dolls! In your imagination you used to live in a world of your toys and comic characters and they used to speak to you. Each of you had moments like those when you could see the imaginary world around you as though it was as real as anything else. However, as you grow up this innate wonderful ability to visualize reduced.

There was a wonderful story in one of the Rhonda Byrne's books where a kid had lost his little dog and the family was feeling devastated. They were aware of the Law of Attraction and decided to put it to a test. The kid and the family had visualized that the dog had already returned. They set out his food bowl. They spoke to him. They lay out the blanket for him as they always would at night-time. They got relaxed in their hearts and minds. They imagined and visualized he was home safe with them. In the end of the story, yes, their sweet little dog did return to the home!!

"You are more productive by doing fifteen minutes of visualization than from sixteen hours of hard labour."

- *Abraham Hicks*

"Proper visualization by the exercise of concentration and willpower enables us to materialize thoughts, not only as dreams or visions in the mental realm but also as experiences in the material realm."

- *Paramahansa Yogananda*

Quick tips to help you with visualization technique

- Focus on one goal at a time to assist your mind focusing better and creating a vivid image which will be held by your subconscious mind and will be replayed over and over even when you are not consciously aware.
- Do this practice only when you are already vibrating high and feeling good. Feeling good is the prerequisite. So first do something to uplift your spirit. Do deep breathing exercise, meditate, play with kids or your pets, have a walk in the nature, listen to the music etc. My personal recommendation always is to meditate before practicing any manifestation technique. If you visualize not feeling your best, it will be only counterproductive.
- Use all your 5 senses while practising the visualization. Try seeing, hearing, touching, smelling, and tasting while you are practicing visualization.

- While visualizing, don't think how urgent and important it is for you. That is wrong. It gives the signal of the "lack" to the universe because it hears what you feel. So, if you are feeling lack, in turn it gives you more things to feel incomplete. Just relax and think about positive feelings of having it and then let it go. Leave it to the universe to manifest it. And sometimes, it takes time, because there is a right and a divine timing for everything.

- Visualize your family, friends and colleagues happily and excitedly talking to you about your achievement, saying things like "You did it!" or "Congratulations!".

Twenty minutes guided visualization meditation in your own voice

Now here comes the best part that clients like the most in my Law of Attraction workshops - *guided meditation followed by the visualization method.* as they instantly feel the connection between them and the source energy (which you may call God or infinite intelligence or pure divine light or anything as per your heart)

Now what is a guided meditation? In guided meditation, practice becomes easier for beginners as the whole exercise is shaped by another person's voice and instructions. You hear the person whom you actually trust! Because the mind has a tendency to wander, many of us find it easier to focus and relax when our minds aren't entirely left to their own devices. This form of meditation is often led by a real person, or by audio or video recordings.

Now the fun part here is, I am providing you with an entire visualization and meditation script which you have to record in your own deep soothing slow voice while using a royalty free slow background instrumental music which is available on the internet. The music can be any of your own choice. Folk songs, spiritual songs, and mantra chants are all examples of instrumental music that can be useful for cultivating mindfulness. Indian classical instrumental music can also be used, which is mostly composed of themes and variations on familiar melodies. This can be very effective for relaxing the body and reducing stress.

Meditation and visualization script

"Welcome to our today's guided meditation. Just find a quiet place where you can sit alone comfortably for around 20 minutes and if you can, then adjust the temperature and lighting of the place as per your comfort. You can also consider using aromas or essential oils to make the atmosphere more vibrant. Now it doesn't matter if you are sitting on a chair or in a cross-legged position on a floor or bed, just be comfortable with your back comfortably erect. Now put your hands on your thighs or on your knees with palms facing upwards. You may find it more comfortable to close your eyes, so please close your eyes slowly and keep a smiling face, this smile is coming from within and not forced. And in this moment for next one minute, check within yourself how you are feeling, just be a witness to your emotions without any judgment.

Ok, now let's do a quick deep breathing exercise to calm your mind further, which will help you to go deeper into your meditation.

- Close your lips and inhale slowly through your nose for a count of six.
- Hold your breath for a count of five.
- Exhale slowly and completely through your mouth for a count of six.
- Hold your breath again for a count of five.

This completes one cycle. Repeat for five more cycles.

While doing this feel your lungs and your rib cage expanding outwards and when you inhale and feel them contracting inwards when you exhale. This we call the deep and conscious breathing. Now come to your normal rhythm of breathing slowly and slowly. And now relax and remain aware and conscious of your breath. What sensations do you notice? Do you notice coolness at the tip of your nose when you breathe in and may be warm ness when you breathe out? Feel the air going inside your nostrils when you breathe in and coming out from your nostrils when you breathe out. Keep noticing for next two minutes and in between if any thought comes like, "what will I do after this session" or "what's the other family members are doing right now" or any other thoughts, then don't worry, leave those thoughts there and don't follow any thought, simply bring your awareness back to your breath. Don't judge any thought, just be a witness of it and bring your awareness back to your breath. Now I am leaving you with the music for next two minutes.

Okay, now as you are in a more aware and mindful state, feel the sensation of your clothes on your body. Now feel the movement of your belly as you breathe in and breathe out. You can feel that you are not thinking about the past or future, just keep your attention only in the present moment on what you are doing. Notice how the body feels right now. Starting at the top of the head, gently scan down through the body, noticing what feels comfortable and what feels uncomfortable. Remember, you're not trying to change anything, just noticing how the body feels as you scan it from top to down evenly and notice every part of the body, all the way down to the toes.

Bring your awareness now on the temperature of different parts of your body. Your head, chest and armpits may be a little warm and your foot, toe, hand, and palms may be a little cold as compared to the rest of the body. Notice it for the next 1 minute. Remember you are not in a hurry to do something now or after this session. You are simply here, feeling relaxed and more relaxed. Whatever is felt in the body, just be aware of this and don't analyse. And now as you are calm, you may feel the natural feeling of being within you, your eternal connection with the universal energy, with that supreme power which you call God. There is a completeness about this feeling. There can be no descriptions about it, and it can't be explained but felt through meditation. Stay with this feeling of being for a few more moments. If you feel a feeling of sleeping or tiredness, its ok, just observe it and don't identify with this. Whatever images come in your mind, they are just images on the screen of consciousness, they do not affect you. Just keep your awareness of your breath and of calmness and stillness within you. Enjoy the deep relaxation that you are feeling right now, there is no world waiting for you to come back, simply you are here, there is nothing to control, there is nothing to fix, there is nothing to change. Now for another one minute simply keep watching your breath coming in and out of your nostrils and then we will begin with visualization exercise.

Ok, now you are in a perfect state to start with the visualization exercise as you feel an eternal connection within you with the universe, with that source energy that create worlds. You are feeling calmness in your thoughtless mind. Now imagine you are slowly walking on a quiet beach in a perfect temperature and cool breeze. Sky is blue and beautiful, with few clouds floating by. Or you can imagine any place you like, maybe some place, where you have been. Whatever be the place it doesn't matter, all that matters is your comfort and your peace. Whatever place it is, it is so peaceful and calm and familiar to you.

While you are walking at that place, suddenly you see a beautiful cottage with a divine presence and aura around it. It is just at a distance of a few steps from you. You slowly start walking towards that small, beautiful cottage, which you notice is not locked. You keep your footwear outside and slowly enter the cottage. And as you enter the cottage you surprisingly see your spiritual master or the God you believe in or just the pure divine energy's luminous presence in the form of golden light sitting there at the middle spot in the cottage on a small pedestal. The master is a very loving and luminous being and very simple but very special. His presence has a gentle glow and a great power around you. As per his smiling gesture, you sit in front of him on the mat in a cross-legged position. You are feeling his loving and divine presence intensely. Due to the master's presence a powerful golden light appears in your forehead and slowly fills your head and your entire body.

You are now completely filled with this wonderful pure golden light of his grace.

With this source of creation ignited within you, you have become a powerful source of creation; you are now a creator yourself. Along with his energy and grace you can now create what you want effortlessly. Now keep your eyes closed sitting in front of your master and visualize 3 things that you want to accomplish. One short-term vision, something that you want to accomplish within the next 2 to 3 months. And then a mid-term vision, something you want to accomplish within 2 to 3 years. And then a long-term vision, something you want as a life's accomplishment.

Now visualize your first vision and create a vivid positive image of your vision in your mind and see it being accomplished. Hold the image for one minute and see how it feels to have your vision accomplished. Now express your gratitude to the universe or to your master which are one and same, for having fulfilled your vision, your desire. Now visualize your second vision, create a vivid positive image in your mind and see it being accomplished. Hold the image for one minute and see how it feels to have your vision accomplished. Now express your gratitude to your master for having fulfilled your vision. Now visualize your third vision. Create a vivid positive image in your mind and see it being accomplished. Hold the image for one minute, see how it feels to have your vision accomplished. Now express your gratitude to your master for having fulfilled your vision.

Now bow down and express your gratitude to your spiritual master, to that divine energy for his grace and energy. Feel the delight of being in his presence. It is time to leave now. Slowly come out of the cottage. Now you are out of the cottage and slowly feel that you are back to the place where you have started this meditation 20 minutes back. And very slowly open your eyes."

Affirmation

Affirmations are formal declarations to yourself and to the universe of anything that you want. It's focusing your intent on a certain idea, something that you fuse into a phrase or something for you to repeat.

Have you ever driven home from the office? And when you finally got home you could not remember how you got from point A to point B? This autopilot happens when your subconscious mind knows the way, releasing your conscious mind from having to pay close attention. This is called implicit memory and is automatic, and habituated. This is where our limiting beliefs have become lodged after years of repeated limiting thoughts. A popular method of changing these underlying beliefs is to use affirmation sentences that focus on what you want to believe, think, and feel. You see, you are affirming yourself all the time, whether you realize it or not. Your repeating thoughts are what you are affirming, whether they are negative and limiting or positive and empowering.

The problem is that you will believe whatever you tell yourself regularly. If you tell yourself, "I am just not smart enough" or "I don't have time" you will find both will become true over the period. However, if you repeat carefully crafted, positive affirmations to yourself regularly whenever a negative thought is triggered, you then practice a new thought process which will eventually become a new empowered belief. Affirmations will help it become ingrained into your implicit, automatic memory, into the deeper realms of your subconscious mind. The goal of positive affirmations is for them to become habituated and turn into BELIEFS! This takes some time and repetition. This is especially true if the old limiting beliefs are highly emotionally charged. Let's look at this further.

Rewiring the brain

Most of the time a particular person, location, topic, or a thing is associated with a certain memory and always triggers the same emotions every time you remember that person or incident. This association, at a physical level, is a neuron connection in your brain that connects that particular thing to the emotional memory. When we are exposed to that stimulus (whether thinking about it or experiencing it), the brain automatically follows the wire to that particular thought and emotions associated with it. The reason this happens is that the brain likes to be efficient! It is designed to make these connections so that you can quickly interpret and respond to the future life experiences. These wires are created even more strongly when we get emotional about something. The brain connects the emotional state to whatever is going on around us at the time. The best example is music. If you have ever listened to a song while experiencing emotional situations in your life (positive or negative), that song will forever trigger the exact same emotion whenever you listen to it in the future. This is why that song you listened to and cried, when your girlfriend or boyfriend broke up with you still makes your heart ache even if you listen to it after a decade. Similarly, your favourite high school anthem still pumps you up. Unfortunately, sometimes the associations our brain creates, link the emotion to something that was not truly the cause. This faulty wiring can do more harm than good. For example, if in past whenever your parents said to you "we need to talk", then it was always related to something that got you in trouble. So now in the future if a friend or your spouse or your boss says, "we need to talk", you become anxious and defensive immediately, without knowing what conversation you are going to have.

"You are being programmed all day, every day. You can't stop it, but you can determine if the programming is positive or negative."

• *Randy Gage*

Practicing positive affirmations is important, but taming your negative triggers is even more vital. The key to recognizing your negative triggers is to become a student of your own emotions, especially when the emotion does not seem to fit in the situation. By becoming aware of triggers, you start to take their power away. Then, you can practice a new, desired thought (affirmation) about that same object that triggers you, and you can train the brain to associate the object with positive emotions and intentional thoughts, rather than those old programs.

Over the time, the neural network in your brain literally gets re-wired through repetition of these new positive affirmations and you develop a new positive belief which has to manifest into reality as per the Law of Attraction.

"Watch your manner of speech if you wish to develop a peaceful state of mind. Start each day by affirming peaceful, contented, and happy attitudes and your days will tend to be pleasant and successful."

• *Norman Vincent Peale*

The 5 P's of effective affirmations

When creating your personal affirmations, use below mentioned 5 P's formula to amplify the results,

1. Possible:

You must believe your affirmation is possible. You don't necessarily have to believe it 100% yet, but you at least must reasonably believe it is possible.

2. Present:

Write affirmations in the present tense as if it's happening now. Use words like "I am" instead of "I will".

3. Personal:

Keep your affirmations focused on yourself and not on the things outside your control. Make affirmations for your behaviour and not related to other's behaviour.

4. Positive:

Focus on what you DO want, not on what you DO NOT want. Avoid words such as I can't, or I don't. For example, instead of saying "I am not yelling at my kids", say "I am speaking to my kids constructively and lovingly".

5. Passion:

The key ingredient to effective affirmation is to FEEL IT!

The emotional response to your affirmation statement is what allows your brain to create the new wires and reprogram the subconscious mind.

And, lastly, repeat your affirmations consistently. This means repeating them often and over a long period of time. Write them down and post them somewhere visible in your home. Put an alarm to remind you to look at them at specific times of the day. Keep a copy of them in your phone or wallet. And commit to repeating them daily for at least 60 days to see the results.

Now that you understand the science behind affirmations and the keys to making them effective, you have the power to rewire your brain.

"Any idea, plan, or purpose may be placed in the mind through repetition of thought."

* *Napoleon Hill*

Examples of affirmations:

Money related affirmations

* I am a money magnet.
* I constantly attract opportunities that create more money.
* Wealth flows into my life easily and effortlessly.
* I am so happy and grateful now that money comes in increasing quantities through multiple sources on a

continuous basis.

- My actions create constant wealth, prosperity, and abundance. I give massive values to others.
- I create money while I sleep.
- The more I give, the wealthier I become.
- Abundance is everywhere I look. I prosper wherever I turn.
- I welcome an unlimited source of income and wealth into my life.
- Every day, in every way, I am becoming richer, wealthier, and more abundant.
- I love money and money loves me.
- I can handle large sums of money.
- God uses my pockets to help others.

Health related affirmations

- I eat foods that nourish my body and help me feel energized and radiant.
- My body grows stronger every day.
- I release all guilt and shame about my body.
- My health is a gift.
- I am mentally and physically well and stable.
- I am in the process of healing my mental and physical health for good.
- I am choosing to focus on mental and physical wellness.
- I prioritize and practice self-care daily.
- I am worthy of having a healthy body.
- My body is perfect, just as it is.
- I appreciate my body for all it does for me each day.
- I awaken each day feeling refreshed and energized.
- I am healthy, happy, and whole.
- My body and mind are always striving for perfect health.

- I release all stress and negative thoughts about my body.
- I have the power to make good choices for my health.

"Affirmations are like seeds planted in soil. Poor soil, poor growth. Rich soil, abundant growth. The more you choose to think thoughts that make you feel good, the quicker the affirmations work."

- *Louise Hay*

Love related affirmations

- I am open and ready to give and receive love.
- I deserve a profoundly nurturing, fulfilling, and loving relationship.
- I am worthy of love.
- I love myself unconditionally.
- I trust that love will find me.
- True love starts within.
- My heart offers love to all beings everywhere.
- I am attracting a real connection.
- I am loved and cherished by my friends, family, and loved ones.
- I am manifesting a healthy and loving relationship.
- I have an infinite supply of love to give and receive.
- I am radiating love.
- I am inviting abundant love into my life.
- I am connected to the universal energy and love comes through me and spreads to the world.
- The love I am seeking is seeking me.
- I trust my heart to guide me to true love.
- I release all past hurt and am ready to be vulnerable in love again.

- I am attracting a kind, gentle and loving partner.
- I am surrounded by love.
- Loving myself comes to me easily.
- I am here to experience love.
- My soul mate is strongly attracted to me.
- I believe in my ability to attract my soul mate.
- I am destined to be with my soul mate.

Career related affirmations

- I have the knowledge and skills essential for my dream job.
- I am open to new job opportunities.
- I am motivated to find my dream job.
- I landed my dream job.
- Job offers come to me effortlessly.
- I am a magnet for job offers.
- I deserve to get this job.
- I am worthy of this job opportunity.
- I welcome good luck and opportunities with open arms.
- I am grateful to the universe for this opportunity.
- I can communicate well.
- I excel at job interviews.
- My exceptional qualifications and capabilities will take me through the job interview.
- I feel at ease during job interviews.
- I use my time, talent, and energy wisely to progress in my career.
- My time has come, and the sky is the limit for me.

Parenting related affirmations

- I always do what's best for me and my family.
- I am always there for my children when they need me the most.
- I make time for those who are important to me.
- I am taking steps to become the best parent I can be.
- My children know that I love them.
- I am a patient and understanding (mother / father).
- I validate and empathize with my child's feelings.
- I make healthy choices for myself and my family.
- My partner and I agree on our parenting decisions.
- My partner and I make a wonderful team.
- I will not compare myself with other parents.
- I am helping my children make lifelong memories.
- Parenthood is a blessing.
- I encourage my child's curiosity.
- I enjoy helping my children to be the best versions of themselves.
- I am continuing to learn and grow to better myself for my children.

Confidence and success related affirmations

- I am beautiful on the inside and the outside.
- I have the strength and courage to overcome any challenge.
- I am worthy of accomplishing all my goals and living my dream life.
- I have unlimited potential.
- I am fearless and confident in myself and all my abilities.
- Today I face my day with confidence and endless courage.

- I am free of all self-doubt about myself and my work.
- Everything I need is within me. I am in control of my life.
- I am confident in myself to always make the right decisions.
- I have come a long way and am proud of everything that I have accomplished.
- I am confident in my business and my mission.
- I deserve to become the best version of myself.
- I am in control of my thoughts, emotions, and choices.
- I believe in myself and my worth.
- I am good enough and accept myself the way I am.
- I always achieve everything I put my mind to.
- I am talented, intelligent, and have all the skills I need to succeed.
- I love the life I am creating, and opportunities flow to me with ease.
- My potential to succeed is infinite.
- I am constantly achieving all my goals.
- I have a successful life and business and I work with the best people.
- I am the best at what I do.

"It's the repetition of affirmations that leads to belief. And once that belief becomes a deep conviction, things begin to happen."

- *Muhammad Ali*

5x55 manifestation method

The 5x55 manifestation method is a structured system to bring your desires into reality. Over the course of 5 days, the aim is to align with the frequency of your intentions by targeting the subconscious mind. In numerology, the number 5 is related to change. In particular, 555 is a number that represents extreme growth and transition. It is a sign of letting go of the past and creating future opportunities.

So, what do you need to get started with this ancient manifesting ritual?

- A pen.
- A notepad or copy.
- Up to an hour of spare time to dedicate to manifesting for 5 consecutive days.
- A positive mind-set and belief in the process.
- Anything that helps you personally to create a sacred space and mood.

How to use the 5X55 manifestation method?

Choose one affirmation and don't make it too long. Take some time to ensure that you feel at peace in the space you are in and that you won't be disturbed for the duration of your practice. With your pen and journal at hand, start to write out your affirmation on the page over 55 times slowly. As you write, say the words in your mind and visualize your affirmation as if it is your reality. Feel the energy of your words and believe them to be true. Do this every day for 5 consecutive days. After the 5 days have passed, let go of your intention and release any expectations. It can be incredibly tempting to obsess over your desires and think about them again and again, believing that this will help to bring them into your reality faster.

But attaching too much to your wishes can send out negative messages into the universe and make them less likely to show up. It is also important to pay extra attention to your intuition and the messages you receive over the coming weeks. You may gain insight on steps you need to take in order to align with your intentions. Don't ignore any messages you are receiving - they are coming to you for a reason.

CHAPTER ELEVEN

Vision Board

What is a vision board?

In the simplest terms, a vision board is a collection of images that represent different goals. The aim of this tool is to focus your energy on a particular dream or dreams you have. The vision board is virtually limitless in its potential applications, there's no one set of way in which to present it. Vision boards are unique to the person making them; you can use them to represent any dream in your life. You'll often see a large cork board with images pinned onto it. However, there are no rules, make it smaller e.g., an A4 or A5 page or larger e.g., covering a section of a wall. Although there is much to recommend having a physical board, you can also choose to make it on your laptop or cell phone. You can print it out or have it as your laptop or computer desktop.

"When you start creating a vision for how you want your life to look, all of a sudden the right opportunity starts coming true and sometimes you don't even know these opportunities exist, but the right opportunity starts coming true to make these visions possible."

- *Vishen, founder of Mindvalley*

How does vision board work?

Vision boarding is straightforward, and it works in large part by focusing your attention. For example, suppose you want to manifest your soulmate. In this case, your vision board can have pictures of fictional or some famous couples who are totally in love with each other. You can also have pictures of places you would like to go together. You can have quotes to be inspired by or poetry that exemplifies your idea of true love.

Alternatively, imagine that your dream is to own a successful business. Your vision board can include images of other successful business owners who are role models to you, along with some motivational slogans.

Let's look at the power of vision boards in a range of important areas linked to the Law of Attraction – manifestation, identifying wishes and desires, creative and consistent visualization. Then, we will move on to the practicalities – how to make a vision board actually work. Now that you have a better sense of what a vision board looks like, how you make one and how it is used to facilitate particular life goals, let's take a closer look at how and why this technique is so powerful. Firstly, remember that the Law of Attraction tells us to focus on abundance rather than lack. In other words, it's only when we focus on positivity, on gratitude and on what we already have, then we are able to attract more goodness into our lives. Vision boarding can help with this a great deal. Rather than getting caught up in thinking about how much you wish your life was different, you spend time and energy immersing yourself in your vision of what your life will become. This helps you to vibrate on a higher frequency and keeps you feeling positive about what you're trying to manifest. Secondly, vision boards can help you overcome limiting beliefs you have about yourself. Each time you choose an image that shows what you want to attract, you challenge that critical inner voice that says, "I don't deserve that!" or "I could never have that." Having a vision board around, helps to keep your mind constantly aware of accomplishing your life goals. Even when you're not looking directly at it, your subconscious mind will be tuned in to its presence. And the more you concentrate on the things you want to attract, the more likely you are to manifest them at a faster rate. Plus, your vision board can quickly shift your mood or mind-set if you are feeling low, by immediately giving you a vivid picture of the person you can become.

A big part of manifesting with the Law of Attraction is visualizing which we already discussed. Having a visual representation of the things that you want is very helpful. While a vision board might sound like a new concept to you at first, there's a good chance that you have used a technique like this without even being aware of it. What about taking a screenshot of an outfit you would like to wear, and then actually getting it in future. You also sometimes write a to-do list and forget all about it and then rediscover it to realize that you have already done everything on the list. If any of these examples sound familiar to you, you have been doing something very similar to vision boarding for manifesting unknowingly.

Vision board quotes

When you're looking at a vision board filled with inspiring quotes, it becomes a reminder of what you want and where to focus your mind. And when you see your vision board every day, it will help keep you motivated and inspired to take action. The best way to create a vision board that inspires action is to put some quotes on it that resonates with you. So, take some time to read through the below vision board quotes, and choose the ones that resonates with your heart.

"Your vision will become clear only when you can look into your own heart. Who looks outside, dreams; who looks inside, awakens."

- *Carl Jung*

"The future belongs to those who believe in the beauty of their dreams."

- *Eleanor Roosevelt*

"If you want to live a happy life, tie it to a goal, not to people or things."

- *Albert Einstein*

"People, who are crazy enough to think they can change the world, are the ones who do."

- *Rob Siltanen*

"The only way to do great work is to love what you do."

- *Steve Jobs*

"Your time is limited, don't waste it living someone else's life."

- *Steve Jobs*

"Start with one step, just one. And then take the next one and keep going that way."

- *Roy T. Bennett*

"The vision that we hold in our hearts is what becomes our reality."

- *Tony Robbins*

"When you want something, all the universe conspires in helping you to achieve it."

- *Paulo Coelho*

"There is no limit to what we, as women, can accomplish"

- *Michelle Obama*

"What lies behind us and what lies before us are tiny matters compared to what lies within us"

- *Ralph Waldo Emerson*

"So be a mirror reflecting yourself back and remembering the times when you thought all of this was too hard and that you'd never make it through. Remember the times you could have pressed quit – but you hit continue"

- *Shane Koyczan*

"Don't be afraid to give up the good to go for the best"

- *John D. Rockefeller*

"If your mind can conceive it, and your heart can believe it—you can achieve it."

- *Muhammad Ali*

"When we seek to discover the best in others, we somehow bring out the best in ourselves."

- *William Arthur Ward*

"It is during our darkest moments that we must focus on the light"

- *Aristotle Onassis*

"You are never too old to set new goals or to dream a new dream"

- *C.S. Lewis*

"The future belongs to those who believe in the beauty of their dreams"

- *Eleanor Roosevelt*

Since the release of the 2006 book and film "The Secret", vision boards have grown in popularity. Once you have made your vision board, put it on the refrigerator, on your nightstand or at any place where you can look at it as often as possible. Also remember to keep your vision board updating as and when your goals are manifested, and you come up with new goals. It will always be a work in progress!

In my workshops many people ask me if they should keep their vision board private? It's entirely up to you where you want to put your vision board, in the plane sight of others or at a private place. What is important is that you view your goals on a daily basis. One reason people share their boards is to create accountability. At least twice a week sit in front of your vision board quietly and dedicatedly looking at all images and quotes. Reflect on why you have chosen them and feel gratitude as if all your desires have already manifested.

CHAPTER TWELVE

Journaling

Journaling is nothing but writing in a diary or a notebook. In the Law of Attraction, you may have noticed that experts in manifestation often praise the power of journaling. Keeping a journal helps boost positive thinking and you can develop a clearer vision of your dreams. However, if you have never had a journal before then you may feel a little lost at first, unsure of what to write. There are many ways you can journal and rather than not knowing what to write, you can learn techniques that make you get into a flow much quicker and actually enjoy the process! Using simple techniques that we will soon discuss; you can reap all of its benefits in no time!

The benefits of journaling

While it's likely that you already know some of the ways in which keeping a journal can improve your life, most people underestimate the power of this daily habit. Let's take a closer look at five of the most significant benefits that journaling can have on your well-being.

1. Increase self-awareness

When you keep a regular journal, it's like maintaining a constant dialogue with yourself. It encourages you to reflect on what you're really feeling and thinking, prompting you to ask deeper questions about who you are and what you truly want from life. This is a great technique to develop self-awareness which is key to living your best life. Without a journal, it's easy to stay so busy that you don't really know what you really want. All kinds of things and dreams can be left unexplored. Approach the dialogue in your journal the way you would with a friend, you then subconsciously take on that message.

1. It releases stress

Journaling is one of the best ways to release stress. Allowing you to write all your worries instantly releases tension. This is because the very act of writing your problems down, gets them out of your head. It also makes it easier to identify how to solve the issues you are experiencing. Also, you can begin each day by writing down 10 things you were thankful for. So, if you are having a hard time letting go of stress, then give journaling a try and see how effective it is at reducing your stress levels.

3. You will get to know yourself better

Journaling also allows you to get to know yourself better. When we understand who we are, what we are passionate about, and the way our moods change, we can start to live a more fulfilled life. Most people keep their journals private. They are the only ones who ever see them. This anonymity allows the writer to freely express their thoughts, feelings, and their core emotions. By not holding anything back, you can get to know yourself better. As you journal you will get to see what makes you feel more confident, as well as which situations are toxic to you. This all leads to enhanced emotional and spiritual wellbeing.

4. It boosts your mood

One of the simplest benefits of journaling is that it can help to boost your mood. If you are writing a gratitude journal, after 21 days you will see a drastic change in your positivity. Writing 10 things you are thankful for each day will make your life more robust. You will learn that you have a lot to be thankful for and each day is a new chance to discover what you are grateful for. Take a cup of tea or coffee and sit out on the front porch watching the birds. And as you sit, your head wraps around a topic or feeling or even a core emotion. And the words will just come. Writing them all down, will make you feel more in control.

5. Identifying behaviour patterns

Finally, keeping a journal can also help you to identify your behaviour patterns. To become a better person, we often need to adjust our behaviours. It is hard to do that when we don't fully understand the behaviours we have now. By mindfully writing down your behaviours, you will get to identify any possible triggers and see if there are any patterns that emerge. This will then make it easier to see what needs to be changed and how you can change it. Journaling is even one very effective way to recognize the thinking styles which puts you in depression. In my workshops, this has helped many people in knowing and rectifying their unnecessary over worrying thought patterns and negative emotional triggers. The result always is that they can see how clever and unwanted the depression is. These are just your undirected and unnecessary thoughts and emotions. There have been a ton of studies which have shown the benefits of journaling on both physical and mental health. You don't even have to spend a lot of time writing daily to experience the full benefits. So, if you haven't tried journaling to help your mental health, now is the time to do so.

So now let's come to the Law of Attraction part of journaling.

Below are some tips to use your Law of Attraction journal effectively

1. Find a notebook and a pen that you like. If you are a colourful person, find as many colour pens or pages as possible, and feel free to use them all. It's your journal, and you are choosing how that journal is going to be. Again, the only important thing is that you are happy with what you've chosen.

2. Now it's time to start writing in your journal. Make sure that everything that you write down is in the present tense. Every sentence needs to be written like that is happening to you at this moment.

3. Pay attention to your emotions. In the Law of Attraction, emotion is crucial because your emotion vibrates. That is how you are communicating with the universe. Make sure that you are writing in your Law of Attraction journal only when you feel good, only when you are feeling emotions of high vibration. Because when you are vibrating high, you are very close to manifesting the things you desire. After that, it is only a matter of time when you are going to witness the manifestation in your reality.

4. It is ok to skip a day or two writing in your journal as you will be doing the other Law of Attraction exercises too daily. But don't give up from writing your journal

with your pen, with your hand. Of course, writing on your cell phone or your computer is much easier and faster, but it seems more effective when you record your thoughts in the old-fashioned way.

5. Specify a time in the day for the Law of Attraction journaling. Decide if you want to do it in the morning, in the afternoon, in the evening, or before you go to sleep. It is your choice what period of the day it will be, but it would be good if you continue to do this at a specific time. I personally do it immediately after my morning meditation.

6. If you have the urge to write something that's bothering you, something that is not perceived as "positive," then go on and do that. And when you are done with writing the "negative stuff," take that page out of your journal, go to the toilet, say "Thank you, I don't need you" and flush that piece of paper or simply burn it.

7. When you write things in your Law of Attraction journal, remove all the boundaries from your head. Feel free to write anything. The universe will understand, and it is not your concern anymore about how the universe is going to solve your situation and help you to manifest anything you want. Allow the universe to do the job for you.

8. When you write something down, don't go back to read it. One of the most critical steps of creating is "to let something happen." And you can't do that if you continuously go back and observe that.

9. Hold your journal close to your heart before you start writing and after you write and send it a lot of love. After all, your journal is helping you to create the life of your dreams! Treat it as a sacred book.

I hope these tips will be helpful in your journey.

Next, I will break down some methods or ideas to implement in your journal. Just be careful, use only those, that are helping you achieve the emotions of high vibration. Only the processes that are making you feel good should have a part in your journal.

1. GRATITUDE

Use your journal to express gratitude for all the blessings that you have in your life. Count them all, write them all because gratitude is one of the emotions with the highest vibration.

1. AFFIRMATIONS

Use affirmations, but again, only the ones that make you feel good. Or maybe even more critical- write down the affirmations that you believe.

3. MANIFESTATIONS

Write down every single manifestation that happens to you. Everything that you've succeeded in attracting to your reality should have its place in your journal. It will remind you, your power to manifest.

4. GOALS AND DESIRES

Write down all the things that you want to attract into your life in the future. And feel free to write down everything that comes to your mind.

5. VISION BOARD

Make the vision board in one of the pages of your journal, may be in the first page. Use the pictures and photos and put a date when you want that to come true.

6. INSPIRATIONAL QUOTES

Find some sentences or quotes that motivates you, inspires you and helps you to raise your vibration. Put those in your journal too.

CHAPTER THIRTEEN

Gratitude

There is a key step in the Law of Attraction that people often forget to use. They get so wrapped up in making affirmation lists and visualization that they forget one of the fastest and easiest parts of the Law of Attraction, even when they do remember it, they don't use it correctly. This important step is gratitude.

So, what do you mean by gratitude? Gratitude is the quality of being thankful or it is the expression of appreciation for what one already has in his life or is going to have.

"Let's start with what we can be thankful for, and get our mind into that vibration, and then watch the good that starts to come, because one thought leads to another thought."

- *Bob Proctor*

In the context of the Law of Attraction gratitude is a very powerful exercise. It raises your vibration instantly and brings you into harmony with the energy of the universe. Gratitude can immediately transform all areas of your life. A very popular German mystic and philosopher Meister Eckhart had said, "If the only prayer you say in your whole life is 'thank you,' then that will suffice". Every day you see two kinds of people - first those people whose lives are wonderful and second those people whose lives could be better. Now, the ones who don't have that much better life have one thing in common – they lack gratitude for what they already have. What they don't realize is that they can't gain more till they fail to appreciate what they already have. Their lack of gratitude closes them off from receiving more as they aren't grateful for what they have already received.

No matter how bad someone's life may be, there is always something to be grateful for. And as soon as they find it, their life will improve. Complaining is focusing on lacks and limitations in your life and as per the Law of Attraction complaining will attract more lacks and limitations and thus, more reasons to complain. If you want to lose all the wonderful, amazing things in your life, if you want your days to be harder, if you want to struggle to pay your bills or if you want to feel unloved or lose relationships - all you have to do is just keep COMPLAINING!

But if you want your life to get better in every possible way, if you want incredible, loving relationships, if you want to be happy and fulfilled, if you want the perfect health or if you want more than enough money, first thing you should start doing is to be GRATEFUL for what you already have.

"As you begin to think about all the things in your life you are grateful for, you will be amazed at the never-ending thoughts that come back to you of more things to be grateful for."

- *Rhonda Byrne*

Gratitude creates abundance. Complaining creates poverty. Don't be affected with what you see around you, with what you think is "wrong" with your life. See the life you want as already existing! See your life expanding in all areas! Feel alive and joyful and believe things are moving quickly to make your life even more magnificent! You are connected to the creative energy of the universe already.

No matter how your life looks, you have the power to make it better. This knowledge alone should inspire you to be grateful and to appreciate everything, which is around you already and everything that is coming to you. If you truly want to speed up the Law of Attraction, if you truly want to manifest faster, gratitude can transform your life.

"Gratitude is the most passionate transformative force in the cosmos. If you give thanks for five gifts every day, in two months you may not look at your life in the same way as you might now."

- *Sarah Ban Breathnach*

Think about everything you have to be grateful for right now. You'll be amazed at how many things there really are. Be grateful for the smallest of things because even gratitude for them can make your life greater than it already is. Make sure you're also grateful for everything you are about to receive. Think of everything you might possibly want to manifest and be grateful for it now – love, money, a new job, a vacation, a new house, inner peace, happiness, a car, a massage, whatever it is.

"What are you grateful for right now? Gratitude can shift your energy, raise your vibration, and make all your next moments even better."

- *Dr. Joe Vitale*

Abraham Hicks says, every time you praise something, every time you appreciate something, every time you feel good about something, you are telling the universe, "Deliver more of this please, deliver more of this please". Being grateful now for the things you want to manifest, confirms to the universe that you believe they are already yours and that you are open to receiving them. It energizes the Law of Attraction, enabling you to manifest quickly. Let your heart overflow with gratitude. Every day, say "thank you." Say it multiple times before you even get up from the bed. Say it while you brush your teeth. Say it while you shower. Say it while you dress. Know that with each "thank you" you are powerfully creating your that very day and your life.

Continue to say "thank you" throughout your day whenever you get time, for everything good that happens. The key point here to remember is that you need to be able to feel the energy when you give thanks. Just because a thanking thought "sounds good" doesn't mean it gets you into the right vibration. You need to be able to feel a positive flow of energy and resonance with each thanking thought you think. Don't thank just mechanically.

"...and the more thankful I became, the more my bounty increased."

• *Oprah Winfrey*

Sit down right now and write out ten things you are grateful for and notice the difference in how you feel at the end of this practice.

I am giving you few examples below,

Thank you for the air I breathe, thank you for this gift of life. Thank you.

Thank you for the roof over my head and the home I live in. Thank you.

Thank you for my healthy body. Thank you.

Thank you for choice and freedom in my life. Thank you.

Thank you for the wonderful nature that surrounds me. Thank you.

Thank you for my intuition power and my ability to visualize. Thank you.

Thank you for the trees, plants and flowers that surround me. Thank you.

Thank you for this wonderful day. Thank you.

Thank you for my ability to create wealth. Thank you.

Thank you for my ability to do what I love. Thank you.

Thank you for the silence and calmness. Thank you.

Thank you for my ability to feel the inner peace. Thank you.

Thank you for my ability to sleep peacefully. Thank you.

Thank you for the infinite opportunities available to me. Thank you.

Thank you for my ability to manifest. Thank you.

Thank you for my family and friends. Thank you.

Thank you for my creativity. Thank you.

Thank you for my ability to have loving relationships. Thank you.

Thank you for the delicious foods and drinks. Thank you.

"Better to lose count while naming your blessings than to lose your blessings to counting your troubles."

• *Rhonda Byrne*

Science behind gratitude

Some of the best "science" around it is called "Grandma Science." Our grandparents always advised us that to live a good life, "be thankful for what you have" and "count your blessings". And it's nice to know that researchers who focus on topics like the neuroscience of gratitude are proving what common sense already told us. So, our mother or grandmother was right. Gratitude is good for us!

"Be grateful for what you already have while you pursue your goals. If you aren't grateful for what you already have, what makes you think you would be happy with more."

• *Roy T. Bennett, The Light in the Heart*

Sonja Lyubomirsky is a prominent positive psychology researcher and the author of several books on happiness. She believes that gratitude is the key for health and well-being. In her book "The How of Happiness: A Scientific Approach to Getting the Life You Want", she writes: "Gratitude is an antidote to negative emotions, a neutralizer of negative emotions like envy, fear, worry, and frustration. Her research recommends gratitude as both a pathway to experiencing more positive emotions as well as a motivator for self-improvement. Research has found that when we express gratitude, the brain releases a stream of dopamine. Dopamine is known as the feel-good chemical that when released in the brain makes us feel good and happy. The brain releases it when we eat food that we love or while we have a good loving relationship, contributing to feelings of pleasure and satisfaction. In sports when you score a goal or hit a target, or in your life you accomplish a task, you receive a pleasurable hit of dopamine in your brain that tells you that you have done a good job. This high flow of dopamine gives you a natural high, creating good feelings. In short, it helps you to feel good. And you know, feeling good is the primary key in the Law of Attraction.

Learning how to thank the universe and use the Law of Attraction through the energy of gratitude is about shifting your energy. Being thankful is not so much an act but an attitude and a way of being. When you truly feel grateful your energy shifts. You raise your vibration, and you align with the Law of Attraction. The energy of gratitude removes all resistance, and you quite literally align with the frequency of everything you truly want to attract and manifest. Being thankful cannot be used as a tool to manipulate the universe though. Gratitude cannot be faked. Only when you truly focus your energy and attention and deeply feel that sense of gratitude, you raise your vibration.

Almost every single book about the Law of Attraction talks about being thankful and grateful as part of the manifestation process. The real power of gratitude lies in truly feeling grateful for everything that you already have. It is a deeply emotional experience and when you truly feel thankful for something your energy shifts. It is this energy that comes from feeling grateful that is the real power and the real purpose of gratitude.

When you feel truly thankful to the universe you raise your vibration. It lifts you out of the lower vibrations of fear, worry and anxiety and raises you to a vibrational level where you can be aligned with all the good that you truly desire. The Law of Attraction works on vibration and the Law of Vibration is the primary law. The Law of Attraction dictates that you can only attract and manifest into your life that which you are in vibrational alignment with. In simple terms, this means that you cannot attract and manifest something if your energy aligns with its opposite. Most people's thoughts and emotions (their energy) are consumed by the fear of not having what they actually want.

The simple truth is that grateful people always have enough. Ungrateful people never have enough.

"Let's start with what we can be thankful for, and get our mind into that vibration, and then watch the good that starts to come, because one thought leads to another thought."

- *Bob Proctor*

4 ways to thank the universe to invoke The Law of Attraction

Being thankful and grateful must become what you are if you truly want to tap into the joy and abundance of the universe. Being thankful is not so much about something you do. It is something that you are. When you are in a certain way deep inside, your actions flow naturally from that. It is easy to see this with ungrateful people. They will always find something wrong, something to complain about and something that is missing. There are, however, some characteristics of grateful people. You may need to deliberately do these things until it becomes a natural way of your being – until it becomes WHO YOU ARE.

Here are 4 powerful ways to thank the universe and invoke the Law of Attraction in the process:

1. **Say It**

Vocalizing what you are thankful for is the first and most common way to express gratitude. We all do this all the time with other people but rarely do this to the universe. Say out loud or just to yourself 'thank you for...'. Saying it out loud can be very powerful because there is a different energy to speaking it out loud than just keeping the conversation in your mind. Saying thank you to the universe at every opportunity you have throughout the day is a sure-fire way to open yourself up to the Law of Attraction.

1. **Write It**

I've discussed a lot about journaling already and writing things down to help you manifest. There is immense power in putting pen to paper and the physical act of writing it, seeing it on paper, and having the thoughts stream out of your consciousness. Keeping a gratitude journal is incredibly powerful. Having a daily habit and a ritual for focusing on what you are thankful for develops an attitude of gratitude. So, you can write your gratitude sentences daily if that suits you.

3. Feel It

Gratitude is a feeling and not just a thought or an idea. When you are truly grateful for something you FEEL it. It is that feeling that is the real secret to opening you up to the Law of Attraction through the act of thankfulness. Taking a timeout and spending time by yourself quietly is the perfect opportunity to really tap into what you feel most thankful for. Just listening to some music, going for a walk, or spending time in nature are great ways to deliberately feel what you are most thankful for.

4. Meditate On It

Meditation is more than just a way to quiet your mind and to relax. As all spiritual leaders have said "it is a way to make conscious contact with God or the universe". I have personally found that meditating on the things I am most grateful for really helps me shift my energy faster than anything else. Learning how to thank the universe and use the Law of Attraction relies on a clear, quiet, and focussed mind. The daily practice of meditation – even if it's just 15 minutes will help you tap into that energy of creation.

CHAPTER FOURTEEN

Scientific Explanation of Law of Attraction

Quantum Physics – Scientific explanation of Law of Attraction and how it works

The website "https://comanifesting.com/quantum-physics-law-of-attraction/" provides the scientific explanation of the Law of Attraction beautifully. As mentioned in this website the most direct connection between quantum physics and the Law of Attraction comes from the Observer Effect which proves that particles come into existence when we place our energy on observing them. Quantum physics and the Law of Attraction go hand in hand. Most rational people are very sceptical about the Law of Attraction. It sounds very "airy fairy" and like an empty promise. With fewer efforts, getting "everything" is not something most people grew up believing. Quantum physics explains scientifically what a lot of the great scientists like Einstein hinted earlier but could not prove. Quantum physics can help us explain scientifically how the Law of Attraction works. But more importantly, it explains that the Law of Attraction is real. It is not an abstract theory but a physical reality. It is a scientific fact that your thoughts create your reality.

Manifesting and Quantum Physics

It is common to hear the term "manifesting" today. The word is often used to describe deliberately bringing things into your life through your energy. This energy is emitted from your thoughts, beliefs, and emotions. As a human being your vibration is not fixed. You have the power to dictate what vibration you are in by deliberately choosing your thoughts. This allows you and gives you the power to dictate what you attract into your life. This process of attraction has been studied scientifically, using quantum physics and quantum mechanics and it is commonly known as the Law of Attraction. While the Law of Attraction is most widely known and understood, the primary law is the Law of Vibration. It is the Law of Vibration that has a more scientific connection to quantum physics and more accurately describes the phenomena of manifesting. Today I will attempt to simplify the scientific explanation of how the Law of Attraction actually works. Hopefully it will help you understand the mechanics behind attraction and manifestation better. Having a deeper understanding will also help arrange the information in your mind and allow you to use it on a more practical level.

What Is Quantum Physics?

Let's begin with a brief overview of what quantum physics is. Everything in the universe is made up of particles. These particles are in a constant state of movement. Even the 'dead objects' like a rock are actually particles that are moving at a very high vibration that cannot be perceived through the naked eye. This vibration or movement of particles is what we call energy. All particles are made up of smaller particles called subatomic particles or quanta. When energies with the same vibrations align, they are attracted to one another. Plainly stated, like attracts like. The rules of physics are different when particles are as small as quanta. Most of us are familiar with Newtonian physics, which applies to everyday objects we can see with the naked eye. Quantum physics is not so straightforward. First of all, when an observer views particles, they actually act differently than when they are not being watched. This quantum phenomenon is called the Observer Effect. Energy particles behave in accordance with the consciousness of the observer. In common terms, your observation of particles creates them and brings them to life. This rule was discovered through the "Double Slit Experiment ", in which a beam of electrons is fired at a plane with two slits in it. The patterns recorded on screen varied in relation to the observer. This means that all particles of energy have a limitless field of potential surrounding it, and the observer is the one who decides how that energy will manifest.

The Concept of Quantum Entanglement

Quantum entangled is the phenomenon that occurs when two bodies become connected to one another or entangled. The entangled objects act as one, no matter how far and apart they are. They could be only a few feet apart, or thousands and thousands of miles from each other. An interaction involving one object causes the other object to behave as if it is being acted upon too, at the exact same time, despite distance. The Big Bang theory explains that everything in the universe exploded into being from the same source. This means that everything in the universe is entangled, or connected, with everything else. So, for every interaction with any object, everything else is simultaneously influenced. And the one thing every individual has complete control over influencing is their own thoughts. When we think about something, we are interacting with that thing. The Law of Attraction causes whatever it is we are thinking about, to be attracted into our reality, through things, people, and circumstances.

Quantum Physics and the Law of Attraction

You now know that all particles of energy in the universe are entangled with each other, and that all energy particles are surrounded by a field of limitless potential for location, form, and behaviour. Further, you understand that the "where" the "what" and the "how" energy manifests depending on the mind of the observer. You are the observer to your own life! Observing, focussing, and giving energy to what is not yet present in your life immediately makes it real through the principle of the Observer Effect. By giving it enough energy, it quite literally becomes part of your life and manifests in physical form. Quite simply, what you think about shapes the reality you perceive. The energy you emit through your thoughts determines the objects, people, and circumstances that will show up in your life. Being aware of something will bring about its existence in your reality. The Law of Attraction can be observed by anyone, not just by quantum physicists conducting experiments. We have all experienced how negative thoughts only seem to attract more, and often worse, negative thoughts. May be you really wanted a certain car, and all the sudden you started seeing the same model everywhere you went. Perhaps you've had the wonderful experience of everything coming together, with one thing going right after the next, in unexpected ways.

If you examine your life, you will surely realize that it is a reflection of your most prevalent thoughts. This is exciting news, especially with the backing of quantum physics, because it means that there is no limit to what you can manifest now that you are aware of the Law of Attraction. One big takeaway from these scientific concepts around the Law of Attraction is that through the Observer Effect you can bring ideas into existence. Manifestation is not a theory; it is a fact. In fact, you've been using this principle all your life unconsciously to manifest everything you do not want, or you do want!

CHAPTER FIFTEEN

Manifesting Health

Outward symptoms are the result of inward conditions

I am a 5 feet and 8-inch-tall person and I hardly got above 51 kg of weight. I was always 15 kg underweight till few years back. And it always crushed my confidence levels. I visited many doctors, and all of the multiple test results came normal, the problem was never diagnosed. They did acknowledge that it's more kind of a physiological problem regarding my false beliefs, that I am suffering from some chronic stomach related illness and it's incurable. I used to have regular induced vomiting episodes after almost every meal for 14 years until I really started acknowledging it as a physiological problem myself, when I read about the Law of Attraction and started reprogramming my subconscious mind with the practices mentioned in the earlier chapters. Finally, the problem gradually disappeared and I gained the perfect weight. But for too long my limiting beliefs related to my health have derailed me from getting healed and getting perfect health. I realized my resistant thoughts were the biggest road blocker towards my healing. Your negative thoughts can halt your healing.

In this new age, we have heard many times that any disease first begins in the mind before manifesting in the body. Similarly manifesting health starts in your mind.

Louise Lynn Hay was an American motivational author and the founder of Hay House. She authored several New Thought self-help books, including the 1984 book *"You Can Heal Your Life"*.
She had incurable cervical cancer and she came to the conclusion that by holding on to her resentment for her childhood abuse and rape she had contributed to its onset.

She healed it through the power of nutrition and the mind. In her book, *"Heal Your Body"* she provides a step-by-step guide to look up your specific health challenge and overcome it by creating a new thought pattern. This book lists different diseases and physical ailments and what are perceived as the psychological reasoning behind those pains.

Alwaysbemindful of your negative thought patterns and emotions as it can trigger health issues or might have already triggered. By finding the emotional roots of your illnesses you can then overwrite it with positive new beliefs.

"Outward symptoms are the result of inward conditions"

- *Louise Lynn Hay*

When you start dieting or exercising consistently to lose weight, at the back of your mind you may have thoughts like, "Dieting is a slow process and exercise is hard work". These are certainly negative thoughts, and any effort you put from such a thinking premise will not yield you the desired results. If you want the perfect body, hold thoughts of the perfect body in your mind. Be in alignment with universal energy first and then put in the effort. You surely know someone who eats whatever they want but never puts on weight. Subconsciously they believe that they can eat what they want and will not gain weight. The Law of Attraction makes their belief a reality. Don't blame the food, change your beliefs. Food is not the culprit, but your fat thoughts are!

Now talking about some diseases termed as incurable, "incurable" is not a word you should believe in now as you know nothing is impossible for you as an extension of the universal energy and having gained the knowledge now of the Law of Attraction. Let me take a very popular example of Morris Goodman. He is an American motivational speaker and author. Goodman has been called "The Miracle Man" following his recovery from a plane crash. He appeared in the inspirational films "The Secret" and "The Opus", and Hollywood producers are hoping to turn his story into a feature film. He has been a successful businessman and a top life insurance agent in the world. He became paralyzed after his personal plane's engine had lost power during the runway approach. The plane crashed in a field. He was unable to breathe, talk or eat. His spine was crushed, as well as his diaphragm, and he lost the ability to swallow, he was connected to a respirator. His bowels, bladder and kidneys too weren't functioning. The doctors said he would never recover and declared a perpetual vegetative state.

But Goodman, who was only able to communicate through his eyes, didn't listen to them. He set a goal to walk out by Christmas in good health. He just had a strong positive belief, but that was all which was ever needed. He never stopped being optimistic and guided his thoughts to support his healing process. It was a miracle for everyone when he first was able to breathe on his own, then by learning to speak. Eight months after his accident, he walked out of the hospital unassisted.

Releasing resistant thoughts for allowing natural healing

In my workshops many of my clients complain about their health by saying sentences like "I have always had this particular condition for as long as I can remember". For such clients who have lost all their hope of seeing improvement in their health and have developed enough momentum around negative thoughts and beliefs, I don't immediately push them to use affirmations like "My health is getting better and better day by day", because their mind will not accept it and it will backfire. I recommend them to use sentences like "I have had this health condition that comes and goes and has done so for many years. There are times it is there and at other times it fades away". Look closely and you will find a difference between these two sentences in terms of the vibrations they generates. The second sentence makes you gradually hopeful and puts you in a higher vibration state carefully, and then in sometime when you start noticing health improvement, you can start using first affirmation for getting fast results. And slowly as per the Law of Attraction, you manifest the desired health condition.

Through meditation and mindfulness, we get an accurate perspective of why our bodies may express discomfort. Then once you have that wider perspective it will be easier for you to believe that everything starts from the mind. Use the power of your minds to influence your healing processes, obviously along with the prescribed medication by your Doctor.

In my Law of Attraction and mind-set change workshop's

I came close to several people combating depression. In the previous chapters we discussed that depression comes lowest on the emotional scale. Whether you are trying to manifest your dreams, or trying to overcome depression, learning how to respond to negative emotions is an essential skill that can help you to lead a happier, healthy, and more inspired life. Along with medication and therapy, the Law of Attraction can produce productive routes to a happier life. Often, when we feel bad, we have a tendency to think that everything is collapsing around us.

The first step is simply to accept where you are. This doesn't mean that you keep getting swallowed in your negative thoughts. It just means that you are acknowledging that you have lost your higher perspective towards life and now it's time to regain it. Acknowledging this will set an intention to feel better, and to keep your eyes open for things that can help you feel better. And then gradually keep looking for general positive thoughts and after some time towards specific positive thoughts. Remember it's not possible to think specific positive thoughts from a negative state of mind due to a big gap in vibrational variance.

Progress as below,

- From specific negative to less specific/general negative thoughts.
- From general negative to general positive thoughts.
- From general positive to specific positive thoughts.

Here is the thing - don't try to soothe yourself about that thing which bothers you most because it has too much momentum already and you can't move that fast on an emotional scale. Instead change and pick that topic which bothers you less and slowly you will gain control on your movement towards the less negative emotions on the emotional scale and finally you will be able to move towards the positive side. During the worst time when you feel helpless, go take a nap or meditate or do deep breathing exercise.You do the vibrational upwards movement work when your mind is not wandering continuously, and you are able to notice when your attention drifts in a direction that doesn't feel good. Then it's much easier to move in a direction that feels better.

CHAPTER SIXTEEN

Manifesting Wealth

There is no virtue in poverty, it's a false premise of thinking

It has been understood and repeatedly mentioned by many of the Law of Attraction teachers that there is no virtue in poverty, and it should be abolished from the face of the earth. You have all the rights to lead an abundant and free life. Understand that money is just a symbol and a medium of exchange. Couple of centuries before man's wealth was identified based on animals he was having, then it changed to metal objects and coins, then to paper currency and its changing to digital currency now. If you are living in poverty then don't blame it on your education, on your ancestors, on the economy or on the wealthy persons who you think have already taken away all the money and opportunities existing in the world. This is your false premise of thinking. These are just your limiting beliefs which you have created since childhood when your parents and teachers taught you "Money is the root of all evil", "Rich people are dishonest" or "Money doesn't grow on trees". These kinds of beliefs could also be based on the false interpretation of the religious scriptures.

"Money is only a tool. It will take you wherever you wish, but it will not replace you as the driver."

- *Ayn Rand*

God or this higher energy does not want anyone to sleep hungry on the foot paths. He wants you to see successful, happy and prosperous. If you keep condemning the money, it will not come to you as per the Law of Attraction. Even if it comes, it will fly away soon. To grow materially and even spiritually, you need money.

"With more money, you can take better care of yourself and leverage your passion and higher purpose in the world. Earn more, so you can give more of yourself and put your money to work for causes that make our world a better place."

• *John Assaraf*

"Do more of what you love, less of what you tolerate and none of what you hate."

• *John Assaraf*

You always took on these beliefs subconsciously from childhood that to be poor is to be more spiritual and closer to God. It was taught to us that "it is easier for a camel to go through the eye of a needle than for someone who is rich to enter the kingdom of God". These are immature states of consciousness. You have to regain consciousness of the infinite supply of abundance and drop your superstitions. Don't praise poverty. In order to unfold the soul and develop body and mind, money will help you as a friend. It will give you freedom to take out time for your spiritual growth.

To be abundant is a divine urge. Getting rich is not a matter of environment, skill or age group. If it were then all the people of a city full of opportunities, or a group of people with the same skill set or same age group would become wealthy. But is this the case? Absolutely not! Abundance is just a mind-set. You would have seen many people with great talent remain poor throughout life and others with less or no talent flourish. The difference is in their burning desire and faith in the unseen, in that infinite universal intelligence. The difference is in their alignment with who they actually are in their core inner being, the alignment with higher self, which gives you the inspiration to take the right action, which shows you the shortest, fastest and most pleasant path towards abundance.

"Formal education will make you a living; self-education will make you a fortune."

• *Jim Rohn*

Again, to get into the alignment with universal energy use the techniques discussed in this book. Do meditation and then affirm sentences like, "I am prosperous and abundant". But be watchful that these affirmations should not be invoking the feeling of lack and limitations. In the back of your mind these voices should not arise that "no you are not abundant, you are broke and unsuccessful". If that is the case then start with affirmations like, "I am on my way to becoming prosperous and abundant". Your mind will be more receptive to these kinds of affirmations and will not generate contradictory feelings.

"You must gain control over your money or the lack of it will forever control you."

• *Dave Ramsey*

In his popular book, *"The Power of Subconscious Mind"*, Joseph Murphy gives an example of a young Australian boy who wanted to become a physician and surgeon. However, the boy did not have the money nor did he have graduated from high school to start his journey toward doing so. For expenses he used to clean doctor's offices and do other odd jobs. Every night before he fell asleep, he would envision a medical diploma hanging on his wall with his name on it. Results followed as he persisted. Eventually, he got a break when a doctor saw his potential and taught him how to sterilize instruments and give injections. The doctor paid him for this work, and the boy used this money for his medical school tuition. He became a prominent doctor in Montreal, Canada. His wealth was in his mind! This is a perfect example of combining your passions with positive visualization, leading to initial success and motivating you to excel even further.

Also praise others, be happy in their success. We all are connected in spirit and via vibration. If you bless others and pray for them, it's the greatest contribution, especially when it's without any gains or expectations.

Due to the Law of Attraction by helping others, the happiness it brings will have a compound effect on your life. When we put out more positivity into the world, it is only going to bring about more positive people, events, and circumstances in our lives. Without any expectations, truly from your heart, wish for everyone what you wish for yourself in life. Feel happiness if your colleague gets a promotion or your neighbour's child cracks a competitive exam. Feelings of envy and resentfulness will only bring your vibration down and will make your alignment with the universe impossible, because no one is separate from anyone in the cosmic world. So genuinely fill your heart with kindness, peace, harmony, integrity and brotherhood and you will find alignment with your inner being.

Tell yourself a new story of success about yourself

We discussed that as per much research conducted, we are thinking all the time - almost 60 to 80 thousand thoughts each day. And most of the time we think about what we can do and what we can't. So, most of the day you are telling yourself a story about yourself which unfortunately is a story of limitations and powerlessness for most of the people. Change that story and start telling your story in an entirely new way using affirmations and visualizations, till it brings you to a new optimistic mind-set and becomes your real story. Anything you are giving your attention to is an invitation to the essence of it. Consciously create your own reality and control your own life experiences. Act deliberately and not by default.

"Persist – don't take no for an answer. If you're happy to sit at your desk and not take any risk, you'll be sitting at your desk for the next 20 years."

- *David Rubenstein*

Abraham Hicks says the most valuable skill that you could ever develop is the skill of directing your thoughts toward what you want - to be adept at quickly evaluating all situations and then quickly concluding what you want most

- and then giving your undivided attention to that. There is a tremendous skill in directing your own thoughts that will yield results that cannot be compared with results that mere actions can provide.

Manifesting Love

Are you longing for a soul mate, to find a partner who will love and adore you? If yes, this chapter is for you.

Broken hearted to healing, disbelieving to believing

Keeping her anonymity let me tell you one of a wonderful soul mate manifestation story about one of my clients. When she attended my Law of Attraction master class in early 2021, she was desperately looking for a loving and fulfilling relationship which should end in a marriage. Her last committed relationship ended in 2017 as a bad breakup. She was a 33 years old, working and unmarried woman, when she attended my master class. As per Indian standard she felt that her clock was ticking to get married and she was holding many limiting beliefs (mentioned in next page), which she was unaware of, are actual reasons for not getting the desired partner.

- I am too old now to get the partner of my choice.
- I don't have a fair complexion.
- I have a lot of emotional baggage from my past relationships, and I can't be a good partner.
- I'm too picky and therefore won't find what I want from a person.
- I have to succumb to my parent's expectation to get married with a person of their choice which may not be a suitable person for me.

If you are vibrating low due to constant negative feelings then it will affect every area of your life, be it relationships, health, money, or career. Due to her worrying about finding a desired partner, she has already gathered much momentum around negative emotions. This affected other areas of her life. She lost her job during covid pandemic (wondering, she was always a good performer) and developed health issues like cervical and pelvic pain. Eventually grieving became her daily practice. Gradually she became emotionally handicapped, crying between the pillows. We sat online patiently and discussed her problem. She understood the concepts of the Law of Attraction gradually and began with meditation practice first which helped her in clearing her mind and bringing her awareness into the present moment. She found deep breathing exercise very effective in reducing depressive symptoms that she has developed over time. A right blend of meditation, visualization and affirmation practices helped her to overcome her limiting beliefs.

She started affirming below daily,

- I release all stress and negative thoughts and I am mentally and physically well and stable.
- I am healthy, happy, and whole.
- I am worthy of the opportunities that life has to provide in every area of my life.
- I am destined to be with my soul mate.
- I am attracting a kind, gentle and loving partner.
- I deserve a profoundly nurturing, fulfilling, and loving relationship.
- I am motivated to find my dream job.
- I welcome good luck and opportunities with open arms.
- Job offers come to me effortlessly.

On a good-sized board, she glued printed papers with these affirmations. She put the pictures of places she wanted to visit with her soul mate, she put the picture of her aunt and uncle who as per her were one of the most loving couples she had ever seen, and she was very close to them. In the morning, post meditation practice, she sat daily for 10 minutes in front of her vision board, feeling happy and full of hope. Her old limiting beliefs started melting and new strong beliefs started forming in her subconscious mind.

In her journal diary she wrote down below qualities she wanted to see in her soul mate.

- Good sense of humour
- Passionate and loving
- Compassionate
- Open minded
- Honest
- Loyal
- Financially responsible
- Funny
- Happy
- Emotionally available
- Spiritual seeker

She started feeling that she is living with her soul mate. She also embraced self-care and understood that true love starts within, and to attract real connection, her heart should offer love to herself and to all beings around her. Before manifesting her partner, first she found a job - a better workplace and salary package from the last one! Her health improved and she gained much confidence in herself and more trust in the Law of Attraction. Then in the new workplace she found an eternal connection with one of her colleagues, magically exhibiting most of the qualities she had desired. As I am writing this chapter their bond is just growing deeper. Earlier, she tried going to a lot of crowded places and parties on the suggestion of her friends, but only met her soul mate when she was silent, still and at peace with herself.

"If you want more money in your life, give some away. If you want more love, give some to someone else. Whatever you want more of, give more of."

• *John Assaraf*

"Eat like you love yourself. Move like you love yourself. Speak like you love yourself. Act like you love yourself."

• *John Assaraf*

Are you ready to meet your soul mate right at this moment? What will your home look like if you have to welcome your soul mate now? Is it in that state? If not, then start making room for your soul mate in your home and make it beautiful. Live like you are living with him or her. Make space for your soul mate on all levels of your being, in all areas of your life. Creating space is essential to welcome something new. Keep 2 pillows in your bed. Park your car in your Car Parking space with space left for your soul mate's car. Live outside of your current reality, and step into the reality you wish to come true. These rituals will uplift your energy and energy of your home and will send a clear message to the universe of what needs to be delivered! Universe will then manifest what you desire in no time.

"When you want to attract something into your life, make sure your actions don't contradict your desires... Think about what you have asked for, and make sure that your actions are mirroring what you expect to receive, and that they're not contradicting what you've asked for. Act as if you are receiving it. Do exactly what you would do if you were receiving it today, and take actions in your life to reflect that powerful expectation. Make room to receive your desires, and as you do, you are sending out that powerful signal of expectation."

- *Rhonda Byrne*

What is Love?

There is a lot of emotion attached to the subject of Love and lots of fanciful things have been said about it.

One of the disciples of Osho asked him "What is love?"

He said, love is a hierarchy, from the lowest rung to the highest, from sex to super consciousness. There are many, many layers, many planes of love. If you are existing on the lowest rung, you will have a totally different idea of love, than the person who is existing on the highest rung.

At the lowest, love is a kind of politics, wherever love is contaminated by the idea of domination, it is politics. Here a person talks about love but the deep desire is to exploit the other, of which in most cases he is not consciously aware but only aware at unconscious level. Hence so much possessiveness and so much jealousy become a part, an intrinsic part, of his love. That's why in these cases, love creates more misery than joy. This is the lowest form of love. Nothing is wrong with it if you can use it as a stepping-stone to move to a higher rung. During meditation, if you can watch it, if you try to understand it, in that very understanding you will reach another rung, you will start moving upwards.

Only at the highest peak, when love is not a relationship anymore, when love becomes a state of your being, the lotus opens totally, and great perfume is released – but only at the highest peak. At its lowest, love is just a political relationship. At its highest, love is a pure state of consciousness.

"Love is not something that you do. Love is something that you are. Either you can use somebody as a support to make yourself loving or you can simply become loving. After all, it is not somebody else's quality, it is your quality. You are using the other person as a key to open this up. But you can also open it up from inside without the help of the other person. "

• *Sadhguru Jaggi Vasudev*

So, to attract your true soul mate, gradually move up first, till love becomes your being. Start with loving yourself and everyone around you. Your love should be just a sheer joy of giving positivity to others, blessing everyone around. Transform your love through meditation. Through meditation any of the unknown reasons to seek love will come to surface and you will be able to observe them. And observing any unwanted motive will automatically make you more aware of them and those unwanted\impure motives to seek love will melt into your newly found consciousness. And when love is unmotivated, then love is the greatest thing that can ever happen to anybody. Then love is something of the ultimate, of the beyond. A pure energy will wash you in meditation making you a powerful magnet now, to attract true love into your life. Then you will also always feel relaxed, light-hearted, and content in your life. And you will then approach your soul mate search with a spirit of joyful anticipation rather than of need.

"To acquire love, fill yourself up with it until you become a magnet."

- *Charles Haanel*

Keep doing your meditation and visualization practices daily for at least 15 minutes. The more specific details you think about them, the better. See yourself having significant moments such as going on dates, cuddling on the couch! or celebrating your wedding anniversary. As you go through your day, follow your gut instincts, and do take inspired action to help the Law of Attraction to help you. Always create a positive energy vibration around you by meditation, music, scented sticks etc. And in any person, you meet throughout the day, only focus on the qualities that are important to you in a person, you will begin to attract those qualities into your life.

Can I use the Law of Attraction to attract a specific person?

I cannot tell you how many messages and calls I keep getting from people asking me desperately to teach them how to manifest a specific person as their soul mate. I often hear the same sentences like, "I want my ex back in my life because he or she is the only one whom I can love! (Even though they cheated on me/left me/abused me/etc...)" or "I'm in love with this particular person, but he\she don't even notice me!"

Here's what I have to say about manifesting a specific person. Please, don't!

Remember that you can't control the other person's thoughts. The Law of Attraction works in the same way for everyone as for you, so you will only end up creating tension and conflict in any such attempt. You can only control your own thoughts and actions. Every person on earth including your specific person has their own free will. Not considering and eliminating their free will is impossible obviously and unethical and immoral too at the same time. It's like saying - "I need you to love me, so that I can feel happy". Sometimes hormones are the ones who overwrites our intellect and sometimes uncontrolled emotions and the lack of consciousness of our true self are the causes of such desires"

"If you are trying to extract joy, love and pleasantness out of somebody, this is going to be disastrous for both the people. I am not saying it is better to live alone. I am saying the way you are should be determined by you. If this is so and you are here to share your love with people, if you are feeling wonderful and you want to share this with somebody, then it will be very beautiful."

- *Sadhguru Jaggi Vasudev*

So, focus on attracting the qualities that are important to you in a relationship, and let the universe handle the rest. Unless you are manifesting someone while they are simultaneously manifesting you, your chances of success are very less. So, in case the two persons love each other but have some social, family, financial or any other roadblock between them, then invoking the Law of Attraction will clear out any obstacle between you effortlessly without any doubt. Many people contact me who have put their lives on pause for years trying to manifest that particular person, but they don't realize that at the end of the day you want the feeling of LOVE. Allow the universe to align you with that perfect someone out of the 7 billion people on this planet!

Use your energy wisely and manifest from a space of awareness and pure consciousness. Know that the universe always has a better plan for you, so don't stop it from giving you the full abundance and realize the limitless possibility available to you.

Manifesting dream Career

It is not your qualification that counts; it is the clarity of your perception

Before discussing how to manifest your dream career, first let's discuss what do we mean by career? A career is something you enjoy doing and give your best while doing it. Based on your life experiences you get influenced by clear ideas of what you want to do and thus are able to explore your full potential and experience joy in the process. And of course, based on your alignment with universal energy (which is a result of the joy you get in what you are doing) you enjoy good financial returns too. This seems to be a sensible definition of career, isn't it!

So, with this newly found perspective while choosing a career, begin first with setting your dominant intention as - "I want to do something that will bring absolute joy and freedom in my life and my unique gifts and talent will be a perfect match to it".

Be mindful that your choice of career is not coming hurriedly from the need to justify yourself to the society or family, as per their standard of what a successful person looks like. It's easy to make your career decisions from these false premises of ideas of success and happiness because you have heard all the time people asking this first question to each other when they meet for the first time "What do you do for a living"! So, you should be able to take your decisions from a wider perception of life. It is not your qualification that counts; it is the clarity of your perception.

"The problem is people jump into something and then exercise their mind – no. Before you jump into something, it needs to be looked at with enough attention because once you jump into something; there should be no looking back. If you are constantly looking at the rear-view mirror, you are not going to go forward."

- *Sadhguru Jaggi Vasudev*

Don't allow other people's opinion to be part of your decision making; it will put you out of alignment from your inner being. You are not here to please everyone; there will always be someone who does not agree with you. Also, if you are not mindful while making this very important decision of choosing the right career, you will get motivated by factors like just designation or just money that you are getting. Research has shown that for most people designation subsides money while taking a career call and they hardly think if they will enjoy what they are going to do. It simply means most of the people still seek other people's approval to feel happy, but those other peoples can't give you long lasting attention. Also, if you don't enjoy what you do, it will make you sad and will throw you out of alignment with your own well-being.

You cannot fill the void within you from seeking just better designation, money, or a good office place. The tricky part is, once you come in alignment with your inner being, with the universal energy, then you are gently guided towards what you love to do most. And when you take the inspired action and make it your career, then all the above stuff like money, designation, prestige will be a by-product anyway.

This is the Law of Abundance!

The Law of Abundance is a universal law, which states that there is an unlimited source of everything we need or want. This abundance is already yours, available to all of you all the time. You just need to keep yourself calm, happy, and aligned with who you really are.

So, whether you are in an early stage of choosing your career, or want to make a switch, first calm yourself down, meditate for a few days and keep a check on your gut feeling which is nothing but gentle guidance from the universe. Take the inspired action and your growth will be much more satisfying, swift, and effortless.

What is holding back your career?

Don't look too much upon society, family, or friends for direction in your career. The eternal guidance is always available to you once you are calm and blissful. I have always experienced it and since the last few years I don't jump at the action part till it feels light and aligned with my inner voice. And I have got the results that I had never imagined due to my earlier limited beliefs and feeling of unworthiness.

Don't wait for the right time to make decisions. The time is always now; you have already experienced the situations that made you aware of what you want and what you don't want. Don't wait for the perfect timing and perfect circumstances to take the first step towards fulfilling your intention. Allow the universe to unfold the circumstances to lead you towards your intention. Don't wait for more clarity, more money, or change in work environment etc. The key to begin is to feel good first with whatever you have right now, look for good things in your job right now. Make a list of things that you love about your current job. Feel excited about the new opportunities that the universe has to provide based on your alignment with it. In your joy, new doors will open automatically. Observe the universe's response to your improved vibration.

Fun and earning money are possible at the same time. You don't need to live weekends to weekends. The early years when you worked hard for less money should make you aware now, what you want and what you don't. You are never too late or too old to start something new that you love. Don't get stuck into possibilities and probabilities. Start with a feeling of excitement and, anticipation of something wonderful. And the universe must deliver to you a viable means to achieve your desires. The secret of success in any area is just to keep yourself happy! It's so simple that's why it's hard to believe. You have always been brainwashed to do hard work, from the people who themselves didn't receive much from the hard work as they don't know that alignment with the universe is the key to success. Inspired effort and action automatically come later, and it never feels like a hard work but feels like pure joy and fun. Society has taught you from ages that to be too happy is selfish and it can be dangerous and irresponsible. But understanding your personal happiness means you put yourself in a higher vibration where you automatically inspire others who are seeking freedom from negativity and resistance. Abundance and happiness is your birth right and should be your natural state of being. Others who are seeking freedom from lack will also get inspired from you and come in alignment with their inner being, which is the only thing that matters. Your joyfulness - it's the best help possible to others.

People often keep changing jobs, companies, profiles, locations in the hope of better circumstances. And the reason they keep failing is that their misalignment from their inner being keeps going with them. They trust too much on external factors or are not aware at all of their inner being, of their non-physical part which always wants to see them happy and ready to help them. But their inner being, this infinite intelligence only can guide them, if they come in a receptive mode by moving up in terms of vibration.

As many people keep on complaining about money or work environment, many people complain about time also. They have to spend too much time in the office or while commuting. And they feel exhausted to even think of starting something new or even to enjoy themselves. The problem of such people again is the faulty premise of thinking that hard work is needed for success. They are not aware or don't believe in the power of alignment (which moves, people, circumstances, and events for you to get what you have desired) and thus they only know action as a means to get success. And due to over workload causing anger and resentment they move more out of alignment with their inner being and end up getting no or marginal success.

"There simply is not enough action in the world to compensate for the misalignment of the energy. But when you are aware about how you feel and you tend to your vibrational balance first, then you experience what feels like a cooperative universe that seems to open doors for you everywhere. The physical effort required of someone who is in alignment is a fraction of that is required to someone who is not."

• *Abraham Hicks*

You must have noticed frequently the big difference in the success that many people have got irrespective of their low education and the less effort they put in, in comparison to those highly educated and hardworking people. Don't you wonder there is more to the equation? The only and only difference is in their alignment with the super consciousness, with that infinite intelligence, with their inner being, with the universe, with God - and all of these are nothing but different names for that highest and purest form of energy whose extension are we.

Success in Parenting using the Law of Attraction

We are 3 siblings. I am the oldest one and have a younger sister and a brother. When we were kids and even teenagers, we were driving our parents crazy, at least our mother. We played with each other and had a lot of fun but were stubborn and used to fight horribly with each other at home. Our parents loved us very much of course, but when we were misbehaving, we were taking them out of that good feeling place. Talking about myself, I was average in my academics, but my father had highest hopes for me. When my parents used to give advice or sometimes scold me for doing something they felt I was not supposed to do or for my low grades, I used to feel rebellious and act accordingly and felt the suppression of my free will. But when my brother and I grew old and made decisions related to our career which looked disastrous to others, my parents supported us as their understanding was coming out from a better feeling place, from a place where their spirits were up despite whatever the situation may be. Thus, it encouraged and inspired us too and we both took intuitive calls which looked like a disaster to others, but soon they were happily surprised with sudden success in our careers.

When combining parenting and the Law of Attraction you have to realize that when you are yelling and screaming at a child, this never works because you will be met with a lot of resistance. Because you will receive the vibration back that you are putting out (like attracts like) and will attract more similar circumstances. Asking others to change, so that you can feel better, never works. Also, you can't settle the differences between your kids by controlling their relationship with each other.

Rewards and punishment also can't bring long term

changes in their behaviour. You would have already noticed this at your workplaces also. Rewards or punishment can only hide the unwanted behaviours for some time. Remember everyone has free will and is bringing experiences in their lives as per their free will, as per their dominant thoughts. Your children are also creators of their own experiences. Your influence on your children that comes from your own alignment with your inner being is much more powerful than your guidance to them that is coming out of desperation, frustration or worry, as it's coming out from your misalignment with who you really are. Out of your misalignment the harder you try the more futile your efforts become.

Below are some affirmations by Abraham Hicks that you can use,

- It's normal for kids to fight.
- They have the right to respond honestly to the environment.
- I am going to quit adding my negative response to the mix.
- I am going to let them work this out.
- It feels good to get my perspective back.
- They really are great kids.
- We are all in this together.
- I like the idea of influencing my dear children to feel better.
- Nothing has gone wrong here.
- I love being playful.
- I have no intention of controlling anyone, but it's going to be a lot of fun observing my power of influence.

- My children are pure, positive energy beings who have come here with great purpose.
- My greatest value to my children is to assist them in maintaining their connection to their own source energy.
- I like the idea of seeing my children through the loving eyes of my own inner being.
- This will be fun.

When you force discipline on your children you create a perfect environment for them to learn to lie. But when you keep a light and open environment at home and when your children witness your clarity and mindfulness, they learn how to connect with their own inner guidance system and learn to respond rather than to react to the situations. So don't blame your children for the way you feel but present yourself as a guiding light for them, gently guiding them towards their own inner being. This will be the best ever gift you can give to your children. Give your children love and support and create a loving atmosphere for them where intelligence and joy will naturally flower.

" A basic responsibility that humanity has to fulfill is to ensure that the next generation of human beings is at least one step ahead of you and me. It is extremely important that the next generation should live a little more joyfully, with less fear, less prejudice, less entanglement, less hatred, less misery. We must aim for this. Your contribution to the next generation should be that you don't leave a brat in the world, you should leave a human being who is at least a little better than you."

- *Sadhguru Jaggi Vasudev*

Your love for them should make them feel liberated and not entangled. If you will impose your morals and ideas about life on them then there will be very less room for imagination and intuitive development in them which no one on earth should be deprived of. Leave them to play in nature, let them explore, allow them to be curious about everything, don't give them the readymade answers. It's your opportunity to learn with them, to explore the world with them, to see the world through their curious and unprejudiced eyes. Feel blessed having this opportunity to raise your consciousness with their help.

"When a child is born, the first and foremost thing one should understand is that you did not create life. You only worked as a passage to deliver life. So you must understand that this has only come to you, this doesn't really come from you or belong to you. It is just that you have the privilege of nurturing it for a certain period of time. You need to build a certain friendship with this little life that's entered your space now."

* *Sadhguru Jaggi Vasudev*

For your child to become a better person, create a peaceful and harmonious environment at home. Remember children's picks up energy more than words. So in case you and your spouse have conflicts but don't show it in front of children, or if you have arguments in office but avoid showing your bad mood at home your children will still pick on hostile energy. So always be aware of the energy you radiate and don't lose your own alignment with your inner being.

"As adults, we have a higher responsibility to become our best selves, because in doing so we shape the desires, behaviour, flaws, and qualities of our children."

- *Mangena*

Give your children privacy to help develop their individuality. Don't keep wondering what they are doing or thinking. Don't interfere too much; just be alert that they do not do any harm to themself or to somebody else - that's enough. They need space for their growth. Encourage them to ask questions as I said, but don't present them your borrowed knowledge until it's your own experience. Even if it's your own experience, let them experiment, inquire and search.

Another highly recommended thing you can do is to very gently introduce them to meditation and yoga practices, for the blossoming of their true potential and to help them seek alignment with their inner being, with their inner guidance system. And again, I am stressing, you can't force a kid or even adult to do subtle practices like meditation. Though you can make a kid sit still, but you can't force him or her to meditate. You can only influence them by demonstrating these practices and emitting positive vibes which will automatically make your kids curious and interested in these practices.

Helping others using The Law of Attraction

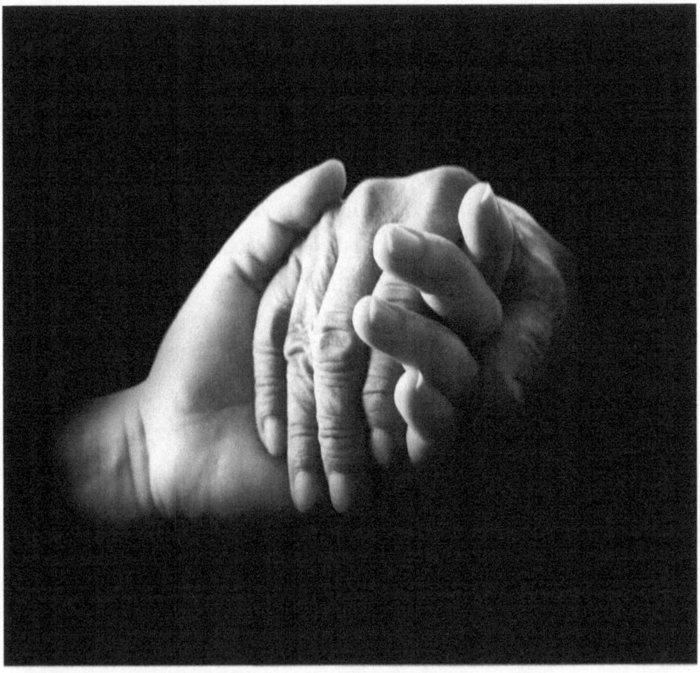

Many people ask this question that if they see their loved ones in a negative situation then can they help them using the Law of Attraction. Remember your sadness and awareness of the bad condition of your loved ones will only be of disadvantage to them and for you, as you will only lower the frequency of each other and amplify the problem. Often you meet your friends, family members or relatives to discuss and find a solution to their problem, but you only end up discussing the problem in more and more details, thus you lose your broader perspective of who you really are. With every detail that you discuss with them, you only help them move away from the solution by lowering their vibration and making them aware more and more of their problem.

But if you don't lose your own alignment with your inner being while meeting them, then you can help them by gently guiding them towards attaining a hopeful state and focus on the direction of solution only rather than the problem. Thus, you can influence them towards raising their vibration and moving step by step towards improvement.

You can't interfere with others' free will; you can't think on behalf of them, your thoughts have no power in other's creation. No matter how much someone needs help, if they aren't willing to receive the help by gaining a broader perspective and getting gentle guidance on raising their vibration, and tuning in with their inner self, you will not be of much help. Meantime, change how you see others. See them as having a magnificent life that keeps getting better and better.

Also, it's only natural that you want to share the Law of Attraction knowledge with everyone you know or who are in need of help. But be mindful that some people will be receptive, and some will not, so remember you can't force things. By doing so it will only be counterproductive for both of you. The best thing that can happen is, if they can observe you when you are in alignment with your inner being and they can get inspired. The right time to tell someone about the Law of Attraction will blossom on its own.

About The Author

Ajay Singh is a certified Law of attraction coach and Transformational speaker, holding an Engineering and Management degree. He is brimming with openness and compassion, and you get the sense that he speaks every word from a clear perspective and from his own experience. He offers transformative seminars, webinars, and workshops on - how to use The Law of Attraction to manifest your deepest desires, to discover your true potential and succeed no matter what your current circumstances are. He understood early in life that to be mindful in every moment is the greatest skill one can have, to get success in every area of life like love, relationships, finance, career, or spirituality. Meditation and mindfulness are the core of his teachings, which are the prerequisites also to align with your inner being and to develop intuitive abilities first, before practicing any of the manifestation tools. He is helping people to get the clarity on their personal definition of success and create lives of greater joy, meaning, and fulfilment, regardless of their current or past circumstances or regardless of what other people want or expect them to be, do, or have.

His philosophy of success is simple:

"Be mindful in whatever you do. Live in the moment and thus, know who you really are. This joy of aligning with your inner being will make everything else work out for you."

Connect with him:

Facebook page - Ajay Singh: The Law of Attraction
Website - http://ajaysinghloa.com
Email - powerwithin@ajaysinghloa.com
WhatsApp - +91 8588843688